ENCYCLOPAEDIA OF INDIAN GOVERNMENT: PROGRAMMES AND POLICIES

ENCYCLOPAEDIA
OF
INDIAN GOVERNMENT:
PROGRAMMES AND POLICIES

Vol. 34
Planning and Programme Implementation

Edited by

Satish Tiwari

ANMOL PUBLICATIONS PVT. LTD.
NEW DELHI - 110 002 (INDIA)

ANMOL PUBLICATIONS PVT. LTD.
4374/4B, Ansari Road, Daryaganj
New Delhi - 110 002

Encyclopaedia of Indian Government: Programmes and Policies

First Edition, 2000

ISBN 81-261-0515-1 (Set)

PRINTED IN INDIA

Published by J.L. Kumar for Anmol Publications Pvt. Ltd., New Delhi - 110 002 and Printed at Mehra Offset Press, Delhi.

Contents

Preface

Encyclopaedia of Indian Government: Programmes and Policies contains authoritative information on about fifty departmental policies and their future developmental programmes.

Organised to be completed in 40 volumes, this gigantic work covers Agriculture; Atomic Energy; Chemicals and Fertilizers; Coal; Commerce; Communication; Culture; Defence; Education; Environment and Forests; External Affairs; Finance; Food & Consumer Affairs; Food Processing Industries; Health and Family Welfare; Home Affairs and Internal Security; Human Resources; Industry; Information and Broadcasting; Labour; Law, Justice and Company Affairs; Non-conventional Energy Sources; Ocean Development; Parliamentary Affairs; Personnel, Public Grievances and Pensions; Petroleum and Natural Gas; Planning and Programme Implementation; Planning and Statistics; Posts and Telegraphs; Power; Rural Development; Science and Technology; Social Justice and Empowerment; Space; States Affairs; Steel; Steel and Mines; Sugar and Edible Oils; Surface Transport; Textiles; Tourism; Urban Development; Water Resources; Women and Child development etc.

Based on the information derived from authoritative sources, this work contains authentic facts and figures. I am deeply beholden to all the scholars whose writings are cited or substantially made use of in the present work. I am also thankful to Anmol Publications Pvt. Ltd. for undertaking publication of this encyclopaedia. I am solely responsible for shortcomings in presentation of matter.

Encyclopaedic in nature, this will prove a dependable reference work for scholars and academics besides those appearing for different competitive examinations.

—Satish Tiwari

Preface

[illegible]

1

Introduction

The Department of Statistics in the Ministry of Planning and Programme Implementation is the apex body in the official statistical system of the country. Its responsibilities include:

(i) Acting as the nodal agency for planned development of the statistical system in the country.

(ii) Coordination of statistical work with a view to identifying gaps in data availability or duplication of statistical work in respect of Departments of the Government of India and State Statistical Bureau (SSBs) and to suggest necessary remedial measures.

(iii) Laying down and maintenance of norms and standards in the field of statistics, involving concepts and definitions, methodology of data collection, processing of data and dissemination of results.

(iv) Advise the Departments of the Government of India on statistical methodology and on statistical analysis of data.

(v) Preparation of national and regional accounts as well as publication of annual estimates of national product, Government and Private final consumption expenditure, capital formation, saving, estimates of capital stock and consumption of fixed capital, as also state level gross capital formation of supra-regional sectors, and to prepare comparable estimates of State Domestic Product (SDP) at current prices.

(vi) Compilation and release of the index of industrial production (IIP) every month in the form of 'quick estimates'; conducting of Annual Survey of Industries (ASI); and, providing of statistical information to assess and evaluate the changes in the growth, composition and structure of the organised manufacturing sector.

(vii) Organisation and conduct of periodic all-India Economic Census and follow-up sample surveys.

(viii) Conducting of large scale all-India sample surveys for creating data base needed for studying the impact of specific problems for the benefit of different population groups in diverse socio-economic areas such as employment, consumer expenditure, housing conditions and environment, literacy levels, health, nutrition, family welfare, etc.

(ix) Examination of the survey reports from technical angle and evaluation of appropriate sampling design including survey feasibility studies/techno-analytical studies in respect of surveys conducted by the National Sample Survey Organisation (NSSO) and other Central Ministries and Departments.

(x) Providing of an in-house facility to process the data collected through various socio-economic surveys and follow-up surveys of Economic Censuses conducted by the National Sample Survey Organisation and the Central Statistical Organisation.

(xi) Dissemination of statistical information on various aspects through a number of regular or adhoc publications to Government, semi-Government, or private data user/agencies, and dissemination of data, on request, to United Nations Agencies like United Nations Statistical Organisation, Economic and Social Commission for Asia and the Pacific and International Labour Organisation; and other relevant international agencies.

(xii) Giving grants-in-aid to registered non-governmental organisations and research institutions of repute for undertaking special studies or surveys, printing of statistical reports, and financing seminars, workshops and conferences relating to different subject areas of official statistics.

(xiii) Functioning as the Cadre Controlling Authority and dealing with the centralised aspects of managing the Indian Statistical Service including all matters pertaining to training, career planning and manpower planning.

(xiv) Acting as a nodal Department for the Indian Statistical Institute and ensuring its functioning in accordance with the provisions of the Indian Statistical Institute Act, 1959 (57 of 1959).

New initiatives

Modernisation and Computerisation in Data Collection and Transmission

To catch up with the modern developments in the sphere of Information Technology, a concerted effort has been made to computerise and modernise the functioning of NSSO by attempting an On-line Transmission of Survey Data to Processing Centres and Modernisation of Method of Data collection. During the 54th round of Socio-

Economic Survey, the use of Palm Top Computers was continued; on trial basis in the States of Orissa & Maharashtra. The response was of mixed nature. Some constraints were experienced in respect of size of the schedules and development of software, etc. An upgradation of the existing hardware and software has been undertaken during the year. With this end in view increasing of hard disk capacity, enhancement of RAM, installation of modems and introduction of E-mail services have been taken up and efforts are afoot to equip the Zonal/Regional Offices with Window based MS Office application software which is more common and user friendly. Steps have also been taken to motivate and train the staff to optimise the use of modern equipments.

In order to encourage the use of Hindi in the field offices, 30 regional offices have been equipped with bilingual software AKSHAR II in addition to the six zonal offices. Since, the power supply in most of areas of the country is erratic, all the field offices have been equipped with OFF LINE UPS OF 1 KVA capacity with 30 minutes battery back up.

National Advisory Board on Statistics

The National Advisory Board on Statistics (NABS), an apex body to provide an overall perspective for statistical development and for suggesting priority areas was reconstituted on 27.2.98 keeping in view to include prominent experts for securing valuable inputs required to strengthen the entire statistical system. Its eleventh meeting was held on 30.3.98 at Institute of Applied Manpower Research (IAMR), New Delhi under the Chairmanship of Secretary (Statistics) to discuss the following agenda:

i. Policy relating to release of data.

ii. Preparation of state-wise index of Industrial Production.

iii. Informal Sector Statistics and Economic Censuses.

iv. Improvement of Statistics on Gender Issues.

v. Establishment of Statistical Authority in India.

vi. Reconsideration of the positioning of the Organisational set up of the Registrar General of India.

The meeting was adjourned after discussing agenda items (i) to (iii) due to lack of time. The meeting was reconvened on 12.5.98 under the chairmanship of Shri Ram Naik, Hon'ble Minister of State for Railways, Parliamentary Affairs and Planning & Programme Implementation at Vigyan Bhawan (Annexe), New Delhi.

The 12th Meeting of the National Advisory Board on Statistics (NABS) was held on 12 November, 1999 at Vigyan Bhawan (Annexe), New Delhi under the chairmanship of Shri Ram Naik, Hon'ble Minister of State for Planning & Programme Implementation to discuss the following agenda items:

i. Action taken report on the implementation of recommendation of the meeting of NABS held on 30th March, 1998 and 12th May, 1998.

ii. Improvement of statistics on Gender Issues.

iii. Establishment of Statistical Authority in India.

iv. Development of Environment Statistics.

v. Corrections in GVO (Agriculture) on the basis of ICS data.

Appointment of liaison officers

The Department of Statistics is charged with the responsibility of coordination the statistical activities with a view to identify gaps in data availability and avoidance of duplication of work. The Govt. of India has amended the Allocation of Business Rules, 1961 in January, 1997 and notified the Department of Statistics "to act as the nodal agency for planning integrated development of statistical system in India".

The Department of Statistics has appointed the senior officers of the Department to act as liaison officers for the States/UTs and all the Ministries/Departments of Govt. of India in order to maintain close liaison with them for effective coordination in all statistics-related matters. They are expected to collect the copies of the publications brought out by the State/UTs Govts. and Central Ministries/Departments of Govt. of India from time to time and also familiarise themselves with the concepts and methodology in use in the concerned organisations.

In the interest of smooth functioning of this initiative, the counter-part officials as nodal officers from State/UTs Govts. and Central Ministries/Department of Govt. of India were appointed by the respective State Govts/UTs and Central Ministries for full coordination. This effort is expected to lead to considerable strengthening and improvement in the Statistical System presently operating in the country.

International Commitment of Special Data Dissemination Standards (SDDS)

The Government of India have subscribed to the Special Data Dissemination Standards (SDDS) of International Monetary Fund (IMF) on dissemination of economic and financial data w.e.f 1.1.97. Whereas the Ministry of Finance is the nodal agency to coordinate the SDDS related activities, the Deptt. of Statistics has the responsibility for the coordination of real sector data categories comprising of Grow Domestic Product (GDP) Production Index, Prices and Labour Market. According to these commitments, India is required to i.) introduce

GDP estimates at quarterly intervals with a timeliness of one quarter; ii) the monthly index of industrial production with a timeliness of 6 weeks; iii) the price indices at monthly intervals with a timeliness of one month; and iv) the data on employment, unemployment and wage rates at quarterly intervals with a timeliness of one quarter. Due to the intense efforts of the Department during the last one year, India has met all these requirements, with the exception of data category stated at iv) above.

For this data category, India has exercised the "as relevant" option, pending the introduction of quarterly surveys on employment and unemployment. As per SDDS commitment quarterly GDP estimates for the quarter Jan.-March 1999 should be released by the end of June 1999. Department has already developed necessary methodology, conducted pilot studies and is fully ready to come out with the quarterly GDP estimates for the first quarter of the year 1999 within the prescribed time limit i.e. by the end of June 1999.

Revised series of national accounts statistics

A comprehensive review of the available alternative data sources and methodology for estimation of national income and related macro-economic aggregates was undertaken to make improvements in the estimates in terms of coverage including implementation of the recommendations of the 1993 System of National Accounts (SNA) and to revise the base year (for the constant price series) from 1980-81 to a more recent year.

Estimate of the working force is one of the basic information required for changing the base year of the National Accounts Statistics. Even though the basic population total and its distribution is available through decennial population census but the trends in distribution of the population into various economic activities is also available through the quenquennial surveys of the National Sample Survey (NSS) Organization on employment. It has been seen that the NSS captures better, the economic activities of people particularly those of women.

Results of 50th Round of NSS (for the year 1993-94) have been used for estimating the work force numbers for use in the New series of national accounts. The base year of the National Accounts Statistics has now been changed to 1993-94. Methodological review improvement in coverage, use of more recent data sources and incorporation of the recommendations of the 1993 SNA, specially accounting for the production of the households for own-account consumption, has resulted in the revision of the estimates in the 1993-94 series.

Standardisation of classiflication

National Industrial Classification 1987 (NIC-87) is in vogue for collection, compilation and dissemination of statistical data of all economic activities in India. Since 1987, sigaificant changes took place in the organisation and structure of industries resulting in diversification and changes in product-mix of establishments/enterprises. This coupled with the release of International Standard Industrial Classification ISIC-1990 Rev. 3 by the United Nation Statistical Division, necessitated revision of the NIC-1987.

To accomplish this task of revising the NIC-1987 consistent with the ISIC-1990 Rev. 3, the Central Statistical Organisation constituted a Steering Committee in November 1997, under the Chairmanship of Director General, CSO. The Steering Committee.constituted five subject specific groups to cover all the sectors of the economy. The consolidated report on NIC-1998 prepared on the basis of draft classifications attempted by the subject specific sub-groups was circulated for comments of various Departments of Government of India, all State DESs, user organisations, Research Institutes, Manufacturer's Associations and the members of Steering Committee.

The feed back was examined and the suggestions/ comments thereon were deliberated thread-bare in the penultimate meeting of the Steening Committee and the draft report was modified accordingly. The Steering Committee in its final meeting held in October, 1998 finalised and adopted the revised classification termed as National Industrial Classification, 1998 (NIC-98).

The report of NIC-98 has been published and send to all user agencies with the request to use the same for data collection as well as data processing in future. One of the significant features of NIC-98 is that it embraces ISIC Rev. 3 structure upto 4-digit level in to-to and is extended to 5-digit level to suit the national requirements. The NIC-1998 has also linkages with Harmonised Commodity Description and Coding System (HS) 1986 similar to ISIC Rev.3. This will particularly help in co-relating the activity data with data available from other classifications.

Conduct of economic censuses & surveys

Economic Censuses and Surveys conducted by the Department of Statistics are intended to bridge the data gaps in the informal sectors of the Indian Economy. So far, three Economic Censuses have been conducted and the Fourth Economic Census is in progress.

The Fourth Census covered both agricultural and non-agricultural activities and shall provide basic information on location, type of activity, nature of operation and employment etc. in the un-organised activities. The data shall also help to assess the impact of liberalisation aspects introduced in the economy. The field work has already been completed in all the States/UTs except Andhra Pradesh.

Compilation of state level Indices

In pursuance of the assurance given by the Prime Minister in Parliament in April 1993, the Technical Advisory Committee, constituted in June 1995 to examine all the technical aspects relating to Compilation of Comparable State level IIPs, submitted its report in June, 1998. As a part of the implementation of the recommendations of the TAC, a set of revised guidelines on the subject have been issued to the State DESs alongwith requisite data for identification of item basket and preparation of weighting diagram.

A workshop of DESs was also organised in CSO on 19-20 November, 1998 to orient them on the concepts, methodology and various issues involved with the compilation of comparable State level IIPs.

Environmental statistics

Environment Statistics is a multi disciplinary concept encompassing different subject areas. The data on these subject areas are available with different organisations dealing with the respective subjects. It is, therefore, necessary to develop an efficient environmental statistical system that can regularly make available Environment Statistics with inputs on all the above aspects.

Recognising the importance of the need of environmental statistical system, the Department of Statistics created Environment Statistics Unit in Central Statistical Organisation during Eighth Plan which is further being strengthened during the Ninth five Year Plan.

National policy on dissemination of statistical data

A National Policy on Dissemination of Statistical Data has been approved by the Government. The elements of policy contain details like pricing of data, nodal agency for dissemination of official statistics, and other aspects like confidentiality, unit level of data etc. The Policy has been communicated to the Ministries/Departments.

Highlights

The 54th round of NSS (January-June 1998) was devoted to Common Property Resources, Sanitation & Hygiene and Services including the household Consumer Expenditure inquiry. It may be mentioned that information on common property resources, both at the household level as well as village level, has been collected for the first time in the NSS, whereas some information on sanitation and hygiene as well as services were collected in the earlier NSS rounds, viz. 49th, 47th and 44th rounds.

Apart from the usual listing schedule (used for listing of households in the sample villages/blocks and drawing a sample of households therefrom), three schedules were used for collecting detailed information : schedules 3.3 (village schedule) for information on Common Property Resources and village facilities, schedule 31 (household schedule) for collecting data on Common Property Resources, Sanitation & Hygiene and Services from the households; and Schedule 1.0 for collecting data on Consumer Expenditure of the households.

All States and UTs except Andaman & Nicobar Islands, Dadra Nagar Haveli and Lakshadweep participated in NSS 54th round at least on equal matching basis. The all-India sample size for the Central Sample was 7030 FSUs (Village in the rural areas and

UFS blocks in the urban areas) and for States Sample it was 7992 FSUs.

The field work of the allotted samples for Central Samples has been completed and dispatched to the designated branches of the Data Processing Division for processing.

The 4th Economic Census was carried out by the State/UT Governments for listing all non-agricultural enterprises in the country during March-August, 1998. The NSSO, through its Field Operations Division, carried out a Post Enumeration Check (PEC) of the Economic Census 1998.

The PEC was taken up in two villages and two urban UFS blocks in each district, immediately after the completion of the main Economic Census. Analysis of data thrown up by the post enumeration check is under progress and will indicate the extent, if any, of under reporting/count of enterprises in the Economic Census 1998.

As per the proposal given by the National Accounts Division (NAD), CSO, a special survey on enterprises covering 14 non-agricultural activities has been taken up by the NSSO from 17th August, 1998 to estimate the total value added as well as value added per worker by these activities at one point of time. The survey will continue till 30th June, 1999. The total no. of FSU's which will be canvassed are 14588, its rural -urban break-up being 6944 & 7644 respectively.

1.23 Efforts have been made for concurrent processing of data and reports based on NSS 53rd round (January - December, 1997) survey devoted to unorganised trade, covering the Own account trading enterprises and Non-directory trading establishments. Data on the usual survey on Consumer Expenditure have been released during the year. Keeping in view the fact that easy accessibility of data (both published and unpublished) will encourage the research studies and in depth analysis of various aspects of the Socio-economic life of Indian population, a National Policy on Dissemination of Statistical Data was formulated and the Government has approved the same on 9th September 1998.

The policy was announced in a press conference held on 14th September, 1998. The policy comes into force with immediate effect. The salient features of the policy are as under : -

i. The Department of Statistics will be the nodal agency for dissemination of official statistics produced by Central Government Ministries and Departments.

ii. No data, which are considered by the concerned official data source agency to be of sensitive nature and the supply of which may be prejudicial to the interest, integrity and security of the nation, would be supplied.

iii. Survey results/data should be made available to the data users in India and abroad simultaneously after the expiry of 3 years from the completion of the field work or after the reports based on survey data are released, whichever is earlier.

iv. Price of data to be supplied should include the cost of stationery, computer consumable and computer time for sorting information. However, cost of collection and validation of data will not be charged.

v. Data users will give an undertaking in the prescribed form to the effect, inter-alia, that the official statistics obtained by him for his own declared use will not be passed on with or without profit to any other data user or disseminator of data with or without commercial, purpose.

vi. Data users will have to acknowledge the data sources in their research work based on official statistics. One copy of the research study along with short summary of conclusions, if required, by the concerned data source agency, should be supplied in the form of hard copy or on electronic media, free of cost.

The concerned subject matter, Ministries and Department of the Central Government will be the final authority on issues arising out of this policy with a view to resolving any dispute between a data user and a data source agency.

Reports brought out by the National Sample Survey Organisation (NSSO), on the basis of recent survey results are being sold both on magnetic media and in the form of hard copies at reasonable prices. The primary data collected/compiled by the NSSO are also being sold on magnetic media to individuals/institutions.

The Secretary, Department of Statistics, held a function on 24th August, 1998 for releasing the publications viz. "Counting the Poor" by Prof. Amaresh Dubey and Prof. Subhashish Gangopadhyay and "Changing Pattern of Consumption in India and some selected States" by Dr. P.D. Joshi, at Conference Hall, Institute of Applied Manpower Research, New Delhi.

Data needs of the Government have undergone many changes since the reorganisation and setting up of National Sample Survey Organisation (NSSO) in 1970. However, the basic structure of NSSO and the Governing Council to govern the functions of NSSO have been more or less static. Keeping in view the changing needs of data users, an Expert Committee has been constituted to review the functioning of NSSO, including the present structure, so as to be more effective in meeting the increasing and changing data needs of planners and policy makers.

Economic trends

Growth of the economy

The Gross Domestic Product (GDP) at constant (1993-94) prices registered a growth of 5.0 percent in 1997-98 as compared to 7.8 percent in 1996-97. The estimated per capita income in real terms showed a growth of 3.0 percent during 1997-98. During the period 1993-94 to 1997-98, the average annual growth rates of GDP and per capita income at constant prices were 7.1 and 5.2 percent respectively. As per the advance estimates for 1998-99 the GDP and per capita income in real terms is expected to register a growth rate of 5.8 percent and 4.0 per cent respectively.

The rates of Gross Domestic Savings (GDS) and Gross Domestic Capital Formation (GDCF) in 1997-98 were 23.1 percent and 24.8 percent respectively as compared to 24.4 percent and 25.7 percent in 1996-97. The share of Private Final Consumption Expenditure (PFCE) at current prices in 1997-98 was 61.4 percent of GDP at market prices as against 62.9 percent during the year 1996-97.

The pattern of saving, viz. by broad sectors of household private corporate and public sectors, has undergone a change during the period. The household sector formed, throughout, a major share in the total domestic saving. The share in 1997-98 was 79.2 percent compared to 82.1 percent in 1993-94. The relative share of private corporate sector has registered an increase from 15.5 per cent in 1993-94 to 16.3 percent in 1997-98 and the share of public sector has shown an increase from 2.4 percent in 1993-94 to 4.5 percent in 1997-98.

As regards Capital Formation by industry of use, it is observed that at constant (1993-94) prices, the share of agriculture in total Capital formation has declined from 8.6 percent in 1993-94 to 7.9 percent in 1997-98. The share of manufacturing has increased from 31.4 percent to 44.3 percent and that of other industries declined from 60.0 percent to 47.8 percent.

Industrial production

In order to capture the structural changes in the Industrial Sector, The Department has launched revised all-India index of Industrial Production with base 1993-94. Recognising the significant growth of the unorganised manufacturing sector the weighting diagram of the revised series has taken into account the contribution of the unorganised sector also alongwith the organised manufacturing sector, for the first time. The revised series has adopted NIC-1987 instead of NIC-1970 being followed in 1980-81 series.

The current series of Index of Industrial Production (IIP) with base 1993-94 prepared by the Department is the most up-to-date indicator of industrial growth in the Indian economy. This series covers 543 items (clubbed in 287 item groups Mining-1, Manufacturing - 285, Electricity - 1) comprising of 64 from Mining & Quarrying, 478 from Manufacturing and 1 from Electricity Sector having the weightage of 10.47%, 79.36% and 10.17% respectively in the all-India IIP.

The Index of Industrial Production is released every month in the form of Quick Estimates with a time-lag of less than 6 weeks as per the SDDS norms laid down by IMF. The estimates are also simultaneously being released as per use-based classification viz., Basic goods, Capital Goods, Intermediate Goods, Consumer durables and non-durables. These estimates get revised subsequently on receipt of updated production data from the 15 different source agencies in various Ministries/ Departments/Attached/Subordinate Offices, the major source of data being Ministry of Industry.

The industrial production registered a growth of 8.4% during 1994-95, followed by a steep raise in the rate of growth to 12.8% during 1995-96. Thereafter the industrial growth declined to 5.6% in 1996-97 and then increased to 6.6% in 1997-98.

As regards sector-wise growth, the trend in the manufacturing sector has been almost similar to that of the General index. The mining sector has also depicted a more or less similar pattern to that of the over-all index registering a growth of 7.6% in 1994-95 and 9.6% in 1995-96. There was a sudden dip in growth to -2.0% in 1996-97 which picked up to 5.9% in 1997-98. In the electricity sector, the rate of growth has shown a declining trend during the period 1994-98, except for 1997-98 where it recorded a growth of 6.6%.

Sectorwise IIP & Growth rates

Month/Year	*Mining*	*Manufacturing*	*Electricity*	*General*
April - March				
1994-95	107.6	108.5	108.5	108.4
1995-96	117.9	123.5	117.3	122.3
1996-97	115.6	131.8	122.0	129.1
1997-98	122.4	140.5	130.0	137.6
Growth				
1994-95	7.6	8.5	8.5	8.4
1995-96	9.6	13.8	8.1	12.8
1996-97	-2.0	6.7	4.0	5.6

1997-98	5.9	6.6	6.6	6.6
Apr'97	116.7	134.7	123.9	131.7
May'97	119.3	135.5	128.8	133.1
Jun'97	114.4	133.8	123.0	130.7
Jul'97	115.7	136.2	128.8	133.3
Aug'97	114.3	134.5	128.8	131.8
Sep'97	113.6	136.8	127.5	133.4
Oct'97	121.1	136.3	129.4	134.0
Nov'97	123.2	140.6	124.7	137.2
Dec'97	129.0	149.3	131.7	145.4
Jan'98	134.5	148.2	139.4	145.9
Feb'98	126.9	145.7	130.5	142.2
Mar'98	140.6	154.8	143.6	152.2
Apr'98	113.3	141.3	137.5	138.0
May'98	119.0	140.1	141.5	138.0
Jun'98	117.0	139.9	135.0	137.0
Jul'98	119.0	140.4	137.2	137.8
Aug'98	115.0	140.6	137.5	137.6
Sep'98	108.0	142.1	128.2	137.1
Oct'98	117.0	138.2	129.3	135.1
Nov'98	119.0	145.8	131.2	141.5
April - November				
1995-96	112.5	117.0	115.0	116.3
1996-97	111.5	127.3	119.3	124.8
1997-98	117.3	136.1	126.9	133.2
1998-99	115.9	141.1	134.7	137.8
Growth				
1996-97	-0.9	8.8	3.7	7.3
1997-98	5.2	6.9	6.4	6.7
1998-99	-1.2	3.7	6.7	3.5

During the first eight months (April-November) of 1998-99, the economy has performed moderately at the rate of 3.5% with Electricity & Manufacturing sectors registering growth of 6.7% & 3.7% respectively, whereas Mining sector has shown a negative growth of 1.2%. The performance of manufacturing sector has slowed down with growth of 3.7% during April-November, 1998-99 as compared to a growth of 6.9% during the same period of 1997-98.

The dip in growth in the Manufacturing coupled with negative growth in the Mining sector during 1998-99 has resulted in significant reduction in the overall industrial growth, which has come down to 3.5% in April-November, 1998 as compared to the growth of 6.7% during April - November, 1997.

The sector-wise annual trends during 1994-98 and monthly trends during April, 1997 to November, 1998 exhibited by the manufacturing sector alongwith the General Index of Industrial Production are depicted in Charts I & II respectively. The sector-wise annual growth rates during 1994-98 are depicted in Chart III.

Prices

The annual inflation rates, computed as the percent change of the index for a month to the index for the corresponding month of previous year, using the Consumer Price Index for Urban Non-Manual Employees [CPI(UNME)], CPI for Industrial Workers [CPI(IW)], CPI for Agricultural Labourers, [CPI(AL)], and the Wholesale Price Index (WPI); have varied between 5.2 to 15.5, 4.7 to 19.7, 0.0 to 18.3, and 3.7 to 8.6 respectively during January 1996 to December 1998.

The annual inflation rates as measured by Consumer Price Index for Rural Labourers [CPI(RL)], varied between 0.8 to 17.4 during November 1996 to December

1998. Table on next page and Chart IV show comparison of the inflation rates and the trends in the inflation rates depicted from these price indices respectively.

Comparison of the inflation rates as measured by different price Indices- January 1996 to October 1998

Year	Month	CPI (UNME)	CPI(IW)	CPI(AL)	CPI(RL)	WPI
1996	Jan	8.3	9.0	7.6		5.0
	Feb	8.2	8.6	6.8		4.6
	Mar	8.2	8.9	7.4		5.1
	Apr	8.1	9.8	8.3		5.0
	May	8.8	9.3	8.7		4.5
	Jun	7.9	8.8	8.8		4.5
	Jul	8.9	8.3	7.0		6.0
	Aug	8.8	8.9	7.3		6.2
	Sep	8.8	8.5	8.0		6.5
	Oct	8.7	8.5	8.5		6.6
	Nov	9.1	8.7	9.2	9.2	6.5
	Dec	10.3	10.4	10.5	10.9	7.5
1997	Jan	10.7	11.1	11.0	11.0	7.6
	Feb	10.6	10.8	11.4	11.9	7.9
	Mar	10.2	10.0	10.5	10.1	7.1
	Apr	9.7	9.3	8.8	8.7	6.4
	May	8.1	7.3	6.2	7.0	5.8
	Jun	7.7	6.6	4.9	5.3	5.7
	Jul	5.7	5.6	3.6	4.0	4.1
	Aug	5.7	4.7	2.3	2.7	3.7
	Sep	6.0	4.9	1.5	1.9	3,7
	Oct	5.9	5.5	1.2	1.5	4.4
	Nov	5.2	4.9	0.0	0.8	3.9

	Dec	6.2	6.3	0.8	1.1	4.5
1998	Jan	7.9	9.7	4.6	4.6	5.8
	Feb	7.6	9.1	3.8	4.2	5.3
	Mar	7.2	8.3	3.8	4.2	5.0
	Apr	7.8	8.2	4.6	5.0	5.6
	May	9.2	10.5	7.0	6.5	6.6
	Jun	11.3	12.4	9.3	8.8	7.5
	Jul	13.1	14.8	10.7	10.3	8.3
	Aug	12.7	15.0	11.8	11.4	8.3
	Sep	13.0	16.3	12.9	12.9	8.6
	Oct	14.5	18.6	15.6	15.5	8.3
	Nov	15.5	19.7	18.3	17.4	8.4
	Dec	12.4	15.3	15.1	14.6	6.5

2

Department of Statistics

Organisation and functions

The Department of Statistics consists of the Central Statistical Organisation (CSO), the National Sample Survey Organisation (NSSO), the Computer Centre and the Pay & Accounts Office. The Department is under the charge of Shri Ram Naik, Hon'ble Minister of State for Planning and Programme Implementation since April 20, 1998. Shri M.D. Asthana, IAS is the Secretary of the Department.

International coordination/cooperation

As is being done in the past an effective liaison was maintained with regard to various statistical issues with international organisations, namely, the United Nations (UN), the Economic and Social Commission for Asia and the Pacific (ESCAP), the International Monetary Fund (IMF), the Asian Development Bank (ADB) and the Food and Agricultural Organisation (FAO). Various international Conferences/Seminars/Workshops were participated in at different levels and there were fruitful exchange of views and information on various issues.

A two member delegation led by Shri M.D. Asthana, Secretary (Statistics) attended the 2nd meeting of the Delhi Group on Informal Sector Statistics held at Ankara in Turkey on 28-30 April, 1998. Sixteenth International Conference of Labour Statistics was also attended by

Secretary (Statistics) which was held during 6-15 October, 1998 at International Labour Organisation (ILO), Geveva.

Three study visits were also undertaken under the World Bank Project which proved quite fruitful.

An Expert Group under the Chairmanship of Secretary (Statistics) has been set up to suggest ways and means of modernising the National Statistical System.

As part of the preparations for a major revamping of the statistical system through an externally aided project, a User-Producer Workshop on Modernisation of the Statistical System in India was held in Vigyan Bhavan, New Delhi from 14-16 September, 1998. The opening Plenary Session was presided over by Prof. B.S. Minhas and the closing Plenary Session by Prof. C.H. Hanumantha Rao. More than 130 delegates participated in the Workshop.

Apart from eminent academicians/statisticians, State/Central Government officials and NGOs, the Workshop was also attended by a few foreign delegates from the World Bank, Asian Development Bank, Department of International Development, U.K. and Statistical Institute for Asia and the Pacific.

Mrs. Rajnesh Jain, Deputy Director and Dr. S. Durai Raju, Deputy Director, Central Statistical Organisation attended the Seminar on Year 2000 Computer Problem held at Hotel Inter-Continental, New Delhi during 24-25 September, 1998 under World Bank's Information for Development Programme.

In addition to above, officers of the Department at various levels participated in training programmes/seminars/workshops organised by the various international organisation during the current year.

Departmental council

The recognition exercise for granting recognition to various service associations under the Central Civil services (Recognition of Service Association) Rules, 1993, could not be processed further due to a petition pending in the Calcutta High Court, filed by a previously recognised staff association of the Department of Statistics. The position is the same as was reported during 1997-98. However, in consultation with the Department of Personnel & Training, the Department of Statistics re-started the convening of meeting of the Departmental Council of Planning Commission & Department of Statistics. 96th meeting of the Departmental Council was held on 19th August, 1998. In this meeting, 19 fresh items were included in the agenda, in addition to the 7 pending items. Out of these 26 items, 23 items were settled with the staff side.

A meeting of the Office Council of the Field Operations Division, National Sample Survey Organisation was held at Thiruvanthapuram, Kerala, on 23 October, 1998. 53 items of agenda were admitted for discussion in the meeting and after discussion, 41 items were settled with the staff side.

Scheduled Castes/Scheduled Tribes

Details of number of employees belonging to Scheduled Castes and Scheduled

Internal work study unit

During the year 1998-99, the Internal Work Study Unit of the Department continued to provide its services in areas of O & M matters. In pursuance of the instructions from the Department of Personnel & Training, information on observance of proper procedure in official dealings between the Administration and the Members of Parliament and State Legislatures was monitored. A

compliance report is also sent. Regular exercises to review, record and weed out old records in the Department of Statistics and its attached/subordinate offices are carried out. Two special drives during the periods from 18-29 May, 1998 and from 9-20 September, 1998 were also launched and a greater attention was paid to this aspect during these periods.

Vigilance

The work relating to vigilance is being handled in the Department in a decentralised manner. For every division of the Department, a vigilance officer has been nominated. One of the Directors in the Department is functioning as a part time Chief Vigilance Officer. Though there is a limited scope for vigilance activity in the Department of Statistics, it has been the endeavour of the Department to organise vigilance inspections of some of the offices during the year.

The Annual Property Returns filed by the Group 'A' and Group 'B' Gazetted officers are invariably reviewed as a part of the vigilance activity. The requisite quarterly returns to Central Vigilance Commission and DOPT etc. are being submitted regularly.

Redressal of public grievances

Grievances Redressal Machinery, in accordance with the guidelines issued by the Department of Administrative Reforms & Public Grievances, is functioning effectively and smoothly in the Department of Statistics and in all its attached/subordinate offices.

An officer of the rank of Director has been designated as Director of Grievances for the Department of Statistics. Similarly, all attached/subordinate offices of the Department of Statistics have also nominated officer(s) of suitable status as Staff Grievance Officers.

The Department of Statistics is not a public grievance prone Department. As on Ist April, 1998, 15 cases, received during 1997-98, were pending. 21 cases of staff (both serving and retired) grievances relating to service matters were received by the Department during 1998-99. Out of the total of 36 cases, 14 cases have already been settled and remaining 22 are under different stages of examination for redressal of the grievances. Monthly/ Quarterly progress reports pertaining to receipt/disposal of public/staff grievances are being sent to the nodal Department, i.e. the Department of Administrative Reforms & Public Grievances.

General administration

The Department of Statistics is responsible for upkeep of the cleanliness of the building and for maintaining liaison with CPWD for Civil/Electrical works in Sardar Patel Bhavan. The Department provides services to all the Departments, which include the Department of Administrative Reforms and Public Grievances, Directorate of Public Grievances, Joint Intelligence Committee, National Human Rights Commission, Wireless Planning and Co-ordinations Wing of Ministry of Communication, Department of Programme Implementation and National Authority of India, Chemical Weapons Convention under Cabinet Sectt, located in the Building.

In our endeavour to provide better common services, a number of initiatives were taken by the Department in 1998-99, as follows:

— Renovation of Reception Area and setting up, of the "Facilitation Counter-cum Publication Sales Counter "on the Ground Floor of Sardar Patel Bhavan has been completed. These counters are for better aesthetics and better inter-action with the public. The departmental publications on sale basis are proposed to be provided through the sales counter for easy availability to the public.

— Co-ordination Committee consisting of representatives from the offices located in S.P. Bhavan, CPWD and the Security Organisation of the Ministry of Home Affairs meet periodically to discuss matters of common interest pertaining to general cleanliness, parking of vehicles, general security aspects etc. During the year 1998, eight meetings of the Co-ordination Committee were held. For tightening of the security of the Building and regulating the entry of the vehicles, services of a private security agency have been engaged.

— Renovation of about 2,500 sq. ft. office area located in Sunlight Building at Asaf Ali Road has also been undertaken. On completion, the existing area will be spacious enough to accommodate few more Sections/Units of the Department and ease the accommodation problem.

— The Department has undertaken modernisation of the office space on the fourth floor in Sardar Patel Bhavan in a big way involving an expenditure of Rs.33-Lakhs. It is proposed to provide all the modern facilities with latest computer infrastructure to make it an ideal working place.

— Renovation and modernisation of the two Training Halls of the Department initiated during the 1997-98 has been duly completed.

3

Indian Statistical Service

The Indian Statistical Service (ISS) was constituted on 1 November 1961 by pulling together posts in various Ministries in statistical discipline which were offered for inclusion in the ISS at the initial constitution of Service. The initial constitution of the Service was made on 15 February 1964 and the posts were encadred in Grade IV, Grade III, Grade II and Grade I. The strength of the Service at initial constitution stood at 185.

The first examination for direct recruitment in Grade IV of the Service was held in 1967 and the first batch of direct recruits to Grade IV of the Service was appointed in 1968 who were placed below the initial constitution/ maintenance stage appointees in that grade. Till date, 21 batches of direct recruits have come into the Service no direct recruitment was made (in the years 1987, 1988, 1989 & 1990, due to the phenomenal increase in the strength in Grade IV of the Service following implementation of the Hon'ble Supreme Court judgment in Narendra Chadha's case which resulted in induction of 365 persons at Grade IV level, who had been appointed on adhoc basis as Assistant Directors, etc. in various Ministries and Departments of the Government of India.) Examinations for direct recruitment were subsequently held in the years 1991 & 1992. Thereafter, there was again a gap of two years i.e. 1993 & 1994. Once again examinations were conducted in 1995, 1997

& 1998. The Department has placed a requisition for filling up of 50 vacancies in Grade IV of ISS by direct recruitment through the IES/ISS Examination 1999, to be conducted by the Union Public Service Commission.

The Department of Personnel and Training had been functioning as the Cadre Controlling Authority of ISS upto October 1984 when this responsibility was transferred to the Department of Statistics. As Cadre controlling Authority, the Department is concerned with the centralised aspects of managing ISS and all matters pertaining to recruitment, promotion, training, career planning and manpower planning for the Service. Day-to-day administrative matters of ISS officers are taken care of by the concerned Ministries/Departments in which the officer is posted at a given time.

In the initial constitution, there were, as stated above, only four grades, the highest grade being Grade I in the scale of Rs. 1800-2000/- (3rd Pay Commission scale). In December 1986, 13 posts in the Selection Grade (Rs. 2000-2250, 3rd Pay Commission Scale), one post in Super Time Scale Level II (Rs. 2250-2500) and one post in Super Time Scale Level I (Rs. 2500-2750) were encadred into the Service. Just before that, 36 posts were upgraded from Grade III to Grade II in November 1986. Pursuant to the decision taken on the recommendations of the Fourth Central Pay Commission, Grades I & II of ISS were merged into the Junior Administrative Grade (Rs.3700-5000), Similarly, Super Time Scale Levels I and II were merged in the Senior Administrative Grade (Rs.5900-6700). Simultaneously, grades IV and III of Service were redesignated as Junior Time Scale and Senior Time Scale respectively. The next landmark development, also pursuant to Fourth Pay Commission recommendations, related to abolition of 13 Functional Selection Grade posts by upgrading eight of them to the

Senior Administrative Grade and downgrading remaining five to the Junior Administrative Grade. As part of this exercise, carried out in May 1990, one of the posts in Senior Administrative Grade viz. that of Chief Executive Officer, NSSO was upgraded to the Higher Administrative Grade (Rs.7300-7600).

The number of posts encadred into the service at initial constitution and at present, after the first ever cadre review of ISS completed in February 1998, as well as their distribution in different grades is given in the following table:-

Table: Distribution of posts in different Grades in ISS

As on 1. 11-61		As on 1.1.99	
Grade	No. of posts	Grade	No. of posts
Grade I	8	HAG	3
Grade II	7	SAG	19
Grade III	54	JAG	138
Grade IV	116	STS	213
		JTS	243*

*Exclusive of 73 leave, deputation and training reserve.

During the year, attempts were made to fill up all the vacant posts, including those becoming available as part of cadre review of ISS. All the 3 vacancies in Higher Administrative Grade were filled up. Also, to fill up the Senior Administrative Grade vacancies, the DPC was held and the proposal lias been send for soliciting approval of ACC.

The ISS Rules initially provided for appointment 4, Grade IV of the Service to the extent of 75 percent by direct recruitment and 25 percent by promotion from recognised feeder posts. Subsequently, Rules were amended in 1981 to provide for 60 percent of the vacancies in Grade IV to be filled up by direct recruitment and 40 percent by promotion from the recognised feeder posts. There were also provisions for lateral entries (i.e. direct recruitment) in Grade III, and in erstwhile Grades II and I. At present, there is no direct recruitment except in Grade IV of the Service. All vacancies in other grades are required to be filled up by promotion.

The Department had issued an integrated eligibility list of feeder post holders for effecting promotions from feeder category to Grade IV of the ISS in terms of Rule 8 (1) (a) (ii) of ISS Rules, 1961 on 7.3.1997. Based on this eligibility list, 136 feeder post holders have been appointed to Gr.IV(JTS) on adhoc basis. UPSC has also been approached to make regular promotions to Gr. IV of ISS as per the promote quota.

Central Statistical Organisation

The Central Statistical Organisation is responsible for coordination of statistical activities in the country, and evolving and maintaining statistical standards. Its activities include National Income Accounting; conduct of Annual Survey of Industries, Economic Censuses and its follow up surveys, compilation of Index of Industrial Production, as well as Consumer Price Indices for Urban Non-Manual Employees, Human Development Statistics, imparting training in Official Statistics, Five Year Plan work relating to Development of Statistics in the States and Union Territories; dissemination of statistical information relating to trade, energy, construction, and environment statistics, revision of National Industrial Classification, etc. It has a well equipped Graphical Unit. The CSO is headed by the Director-General who is assisted by 2 Addl. Director-General and 2 Dy. Director-General, 4 Directors & 27 Joint Directors and other supporting staff The CSO is located in Delhi. Some portion of Industrial Statistics work pertaining to Annual Survey of industries is carried out in Calcutta.

Coordiation

The Planning and State Statistics Unit of Miscellaneous Statistics Division coordinates statistical activities of the CSO and provides liaison with Central Government Departments, State Governments and International Agencies. It is responsible for convening quarterly meetings of reviewing and monitoring the progress of Annual Action Plan activities of the department. It also organises once in two years, a Conference of Central and State Statistical Organisation which provides a forum for exchange of views and experiences concerning statistical development activities in the country.

It is also responsible for providing secretarial assistance to the National Advisory Board on Statistics (NABS), an apex body set up by the govt. of India to provide an overall perspective for statistical development and for suggesting priority areas. The NABS has been reconstituted keeping in view to include prominent experts for securing valuable inputs required to strengthen the entire statistical system. The 12th meeting of the NABS was held on 12 November, 1998 at Vigyan Bhawan Annexe, New Delhi.

In fulfilling its coordinating role, the CSO also participates in the inter-departmental meetings of the Working Groups, Technical Advisory Committee, Standing Committee set up by the Central Ministries/ Departments in subject areas of their concern with a view to ensuring adoption of statistical standards on a uniform basis, minimising duplication of efforts and for promoting upgradation of quality and timeliness of data. It also participates in the meetings of the high level statistical coordination committees of the state governments to review activities related to statistical data generation and dissemination within respective states.

National Accounts

Preparation of national/regional accounts as well as publication of annual estimates of national product, government/private final consumption expenditure, capital formation and saving along with consolidated accounts of the nation and detailed accounts of the public sector transaction is an important activity of the Department. Related activities which are undertaken, are: i) estimation of capital stock and consumption of fixed capital ii) estimation of state level gross capital formation of supra-regional sectors of railways, communication, insurance, and central government administration, and iii) preparation of comparable estimates of State Domestic Product (SDP) at current prices for the use of Planning and Finance Commission.

The annual publication "National Accounts Statistics, 1998" giving estimates of the national/domestic product, private final consumption expenditure, saving, capital formation, capital stock public sector transactions and consolidated accounts of the nation for the period 1980-81 to 1995-96 was brought out during the period. This publication also included the estimates of factor income for the years 1990-91 to 1995-96 and the Quick estimates for the, year 1996-97. Comparable data on macro-econoniic aggregates and population from 1950-51 to 1996-97 were included in a special statement in the publication. An analytical write-up giving an overview of the economy as observed in the National Accounts Statistics and advance estimates of national income for the year 1997-98 were also included in the publication. A special statement giving domestic product from livestock sector separately for the period 1980-81 to 1995-96 had also been included to meet the demand of policy makers and researchers.

The National Accounts Statistics were revised by (i) incorporating improvements with coverage, methodology and adopting more recent data sources, (ii) changing the base year to 1993-94 from 1980-81 and (iii) implementing, to the extent feasible the recommendations of 1993 system of National Accounts. The Quick Estimates of national income, consumption expenditure, saving and capital formation for the year 1997-98 as per new series with base 1993-94 were released on 3rd Feb., 1999. The Press release also included revised estimates as per new series, for the years 1993-94 to 1996-97. The advance estimates of national income for the 1998-99 at 1993-94 prices (new series) were released on 9th Feb., 1999.

As per the Quick Estimates of National Income and related aggregates, the economy in real terms (at 1993-94 prices) achieved a growth of 5.0 per cent in gross domestic product during 1997-98 as against 7.8 per cent in the year 1996-97. The rates of gross domestic saving and gross domestic capital formation at current prices during 1997-98 were 23.1 per cent and 24.8 per cent respectively, the corresponding rates in 1996-97 were 24.4 and 25.7 per cent respectively.

Comparable estimates of State Domestic Product for the year 1995-96, for the use of the Finance Commission and Planning Commission were prepared in consultation with the representatives of the State Directorates of Economics and Statistics.

Industrial Statistics

The work relating to Industrial Statistics falls under two categories viz. (i) Index of Industrial Production and (ii) Annual Survey of Industries.

Index of Industrial Production

4.11 In order to capture the structural changes in the Industrial Sector, The Department has launched revised all-India Index of Industrial Production with base 1993-

94, Recognising the significant growth of the unorganised manufacturing sector the weighting diagram of the revised series has taken into account the contribution of the unorganised sector also alongwith the organised manufacturing sector, for the first time. The revised series has adopted NIC-1987 instead of NIC-1970 being followed in 1980-81 series.

The current series of Index of industrial Production (IIP) with base 1993-94 prepared by the Department is the most up-to-date indicator of industrial growth in the Indian economy. This series covers 543 items (clubbed in 287 item groups; Mining-1, Manufacturing - 285, Electricity - 1) comprising of 64 from Mining & Quarrying, 478 from Manufacturing and 1 from Electricity Sector having the weightage of 10.47%, 79.36% and 10.17% respectively in the all-India IIP. The Index of Industrial Production is released every month in the form of Quick Estimates with a time-lag of less than 6 weeks as per the SDDS norms laid down by IMF. The estimates are also simultaneously being released as per use-based classification viz., Basic goods, Capital Goods, Intermediate Goods, Consumer durables and non-durables. These estimates get revised subsequently on receipt of updated production data from the 15 different source agencies in various Ministries/Departments/ Attached/Subordinate Offices. However, the major source of data is Ministry of Industry.

Annual Survey of Industries

The Annual Survey of Industries (ASI) is the principal source of industrial statistics in India, It provides statistical information to assess and evaluate, objectively and realistically, the change in the growth, composition and structure of the organised manufacturing sector comprising activities related to manufacturing processes, repair services, generation, transmission etc. of electricity, gas and water supply and cold storage. The survey is conducted annually under the statutory provisions of the Collection of Statistics Act, 1953. The ASI extends to the entire country except the States of Arunachal Pradesh, Mizoram and Sikkim and Union Territory of Lakshadweep. It covers all factories registered under Sections 2m(i) and 2m(ii) of the Factories Act, 1948. The survey also covers bidi and cigar manufacturing establishments registered under the Bidi and Cigar Workers (Conditions of Employment) Act, 1966. All the electricity undertakings engaged in the generation, transmission and distribution of electricity registered with the Central Electricity Authority are covered under ASI irrespective of their employment size. Certain services and activities like cold storage, water supply, repair of motor vehicles and of other consumer durables like watches, etc. are covered under the survey. Defence establishments, oil storage and distribution depots, restaurants, hotels, cafe and computer services and also the technical training institutes are excluded from the purview of the survey. The data collected through ASI relates to capital, employment and emoluments, consumption of fuel and lubricants, raw material and other input/output, value added, labour turnover, absenteeism, labour cost, construction of houses by employers for their employees and other characteristics of factories/industrial establishments. Field work is carried out by the Field Operations Division of NSSO. The CSO processes the data and publishes the results.

The latest ASI 1995-96 summary results for factory sector indicate a total of 1,34,571 working factories in all States and Union Territories except the States of Arunachal Pradesh, Mizoram and Sikkim and Union Territory of Lakshadweep. The number is higher by 9.4

percent as compared with the previous ASI year. These estimated factories together had a total fixed capital worth Rs. 3,48,468 crores, productive capital Rs.4,56,131 crores and invested capital Rs.4,89,969 crores. These factories provided gainful employment to 10.22 million persons and distributed Rs.45,116 crores as emoluments to employees, consumed inputs worth Rs.5,07,491 crores, produced Rs.6,70,514 crores worth of goods and services valued at ex-factory prices and contributed by way of value added by manufacture Rs. 1,39,397 crores to the national income. The net fixed assets created by these factories during the period was of the order of Rs.45,494 crores. The net income was estimated as Rs.99,634 crores which is higher by 25.5 percent than that of last year's estimate.

The ASI summary results for factory sector show that the number of registered factories increased each year during the period 1993-94 to 1995-96. The fixed capital, productive capital, invested capital, workers, employees, persons, wages to workers, emoluments, total input, total output, depreciation involved in the production process and net value added by manufacture have also increased correspondingly when compared with the previous year. In percentage terms, the highest increase has been observed in profit (96.7 percent in 1993-94), rent paid (65.2 per cent in 1995-96), interest paid (34.0 per cent in 1995-96), net income (33.8 percent in 1993-94), total input (29.9 per cent in 1995-96), total output (29.4 per cent in 1995-96), net value added (28.5 per cent in 1995-96), emoluments (27.7 per cent in 1995-96), wages (27.0 per cent in 1995-96), depreciation (26.5 per cent in 1995-96), invested capital (26.4 per cent in 1995-96), fixed capital (25.5 per cent in 1995-96), productive capital (25.0 per cent in 1995-96), persons (10.8 per cent in 1995-96), employees (10.4 per cent in 1995-96), workers (9.5 percent in 1995-96) and factories (9.4 percent in 1995-96).

The detailed ASI reports are being prepared in CSO (IS Wing) every year from ASI 1993-94 and onwards. The work of CSO (IS Wing) has been geared up in order to develop in-house computer software for data processing for generation of all tables and their publications with effect from ASI 1993-94- reduce the time lag in processing of ASI (detailed) data from 60 months to 12 months in a phased manner within two to three years and to process & publish ASI (detailed) data annually instead of quinquennial basis; and print ASI detailed reports (in 16 volumes) with the help of in-house printing facility.

Introduction of a new Plan Scheme entitled "Streamlining of ASI Data Processing and Strengthening of Analytical Capabilities of ASI Unit" during the VIIIth Plan followed by restructuring the system of work at CSO (IS Wing) has boosted the momentum in the progress of work. As decided, the Analytical Studies Cell set up in ASI Unit of CSO, New Delhi under the Plan Scheme has also been transferred to CSO (IS Wing), Calcutta during 1997-98.

Recently, many improvements have been made in the collection, processing and dissemination of ASI data. These are summarised in the following paragraphs.

Over the last few decades there has been a spurt in the growth of the number of registered factories and consequently in the number of units from whom data are to be collected and analysed annually but manpower resources available to the Department of Statistics could not be increased much due to financial constraints. Thus, collection and compilation of data from a large number of units (approximately 70,000 in number) in a very lengthy schedule have not only led to undue delay in the availability of results but also involve non-sampling errors affecting quality of data. To improve timeliness and reduce non-sampling errors the size of ASI schedule has been reduced for 1997-98 survey. The sampling design of ASI has also been revised. According to the new sample design about 30,000 units will be surveyed through ASI 1997-98 instead of about 70,000 units covered upto ASI 1996-97. This will certainly reduce the data collection and processing time. Also, non-sampling errors will be reduced to a great extent.

To avoid differences between summary and detailed results entire processing of data of ASI 1995-96 onwards is being done by CSO(IS Wing), Calcutta. To handle this work property, CSO (IS Wing) has been provided with necessary hardware and software. An action plan has been drawn to reduce the time lag in releasing the ASI results substantially by March 1999. The ASI 1995-96 provisional results for the factory sector and Quick estimates for 1996-97 and 1997-98 have already been released. The final results of ASI 1995-96 and provisional results of ASI 1996-97 and 1997-98 will be made available by March 1999. Thus, time lag will be eliminated in the release of industrial statistics to users by end of the current financial year.

The ASI results are available to users on electronic media on payment basis. Only one volume of provisional results and two volumes of detailed results (in place of 16 volumes) will be released on hard print from ASI 1995-96 onwards.

Steps for ASI data transmission from field offices of NSSO (FOD) to the tabulating agency CSO, IS Wing, Calcutta) in the form of digitised schedule utilising countrywide net work are also under consideration. This arrangement will improve the quality of data and reduce the time in collecting the data from the field.

Some State DESs process the ASI data for their States

on the basis of duplicate copies of ASI returns received from NSSO (FOD)- State DESs are being advised to modify their action plan in ASI in the light of the new sampling design with reduced sample size and to avoid the duplication of work in ASI at the State level. The CSO (IS Wing) will provide the entire data base as well as tables needed by State Govts. and State Govts. may generate district/micro-level estimates, if necessary, by augmenting the sample.

Four meetings of the Working Group on Commerce, Industry & Corporate Sector Statistics set up for the purpose of making suggestions/recommendations in the related sectors in the context of modernisation of the Indian Statistical System were held on 15, 21 & 29 Oct.98 and 13 Nov.98 under the Chairmanship of Dr. Arun Ghosh. The report of the Working group has been submitted to the Deptt. of Statistics for implementation of the suggest ions/recommendations made by the group.

The following publications were released upto 31st January, 1998:

i. ASI 1993-94 (detailed) in 16 Volumes (released on electronic media and on hard print;

ii. ASI 1995-96 Summary Results for Factory Sector (released on electronic media and on hard print);

iii. Supplement to ASI 1995-96 Summary Results for Factory Sector by State X Industry (released on electronic media); and

iv. Energy Statistics 1997-98 (released on electronic media).

v. Quick results of ASI 1996-97 and 1997-98.

Social Statistics Division

The Central Statistical Organisation (CSO) continued its efforts for the coordinated development of social statistics which covers population, human development, manpower, employment, health, education, social welfare etc., and maintenance of specific standards in these fields. For discharging these responsibilities close liaison is maintained with different agencies like the Planning Commission, Registrar General of India, Ministries of Human Resource Development, Labour, Urban Affairs and Employment, Welfare and Health and Family Welfare besides autonomous research institutions like ICSSR, NIPCCD, IAMR and NCAER etc. The CSO also shared its expertise with various organisations in the field of statistics by participating in the meetings of the Expert Groups constituted by different ministries/ organisations and by offering comments on the proposals, questionnaire, tabulation programme, draft reports etc. received from various Central and State Governments, research institutions.

With regard to improvement of statistics on gender issues, as the most recent data had become available, it was decided to bring out a combined issue for the years 1996 and 1997. This publication had been widely circulated among the Central and State Governments, research institutions etc. The follow up actions for implementation of the National Plan of Action for bridging the data gaps on identified gender issues were undertaken. A meeting of the major data producers and users for reviewing the implementation of the National Plan of Action was organised under the Chairmanship of Secretary, Department of Statistics on 15th July, 1997. This meeting also discussed the issue of computation of Human Development Index (HDI) and Gender Development Index (GDI) for all India and States as well as the possibility of collection and compilation of data with sex-wise break-up at different geographical levels such as all India, State and District. A Technical Advisory Committee (TAC) was also constituted under the Chairmanship of Secretary, Department of Statistics to develop the methodology for computation of HDI and GDI as well as the ways and means for collecting gender related data at different administrative level on a minimum set of indicators. The first meeting of the TAC was held on 5th March, 1998 under the Chairmanship of Secretary, Department of Statistics. It was decided in this meeting that Department of Women and Child Development (DWCD) will first organise a Workshop to identify the gender issues and the relevant indicators. The DWCD organised the workshop during December 2-3, 1998. Future work in this area will be undertaken in collaboration with the DWCD.

With a view to estimating accurately the contribution of the women in the national economy, steps were initiated for conducting a Time Use Methodological Survey in the country. For this purpose, a Technical Advisory Committee and a Sub-Committee were constituted to work out the details about the sampling design, questionnaire, method of data collection, agencies to be involved in conducting the survey, etc. After finalising the questionnaire and sampling design, field work of the survey started in six selected States, namely Haryana, Gujarat, Orissa, Madhya Pradesh, Tamil Nadu and Meghalaya by the respective Directorates of Economics and Statistics in July, 1998. The Tabulation Plan has been finalised and software packages for data entry, validation and generation of tables has been developed. Steps are being taken to process the data sub-round-wise.

Data were collected for the combined issue of 1996 & 1997 of the publication "Selected Socio-Economic Statistics, India" giving time series data on different statistics/indicators of social concerns. The publication was printed and circulated widely among ministries/ departments, research institutions and libraries etc. Data from most of the source agencies have been received for the preparation of manuscript of the 1998 issue of this publication. The preparation of the manuscript is under progress.

The Department decided that Social Statistics Division may get two special publications entitled "Youth in India - Profile & Programmes, 1998" and "Indian Population - Some Salient facts and Figures, 1998" published in commemoration of the 50th Year of India's independence. Both these publications were printed after collecting data from the concerned Ministries such as Health, Education, Women and Child Development, etc. Both these publications have been widely circulated nationally and internationally.

To verify the validity of data on sex ratio from 1991 Population Census, a diagnostic survey was conducted in 5 selected villages of Haryana where sex ratio was found to be abnormally low in 1991 and the relevant data are under processing.

Sample Survey Unit

The Central Statistical Organisation brings out annually a publication 'Directory of Sample Surveys in India' giving at one place consolidated information about objectives, coverage, sampling design procedure adopted for data collection, arrangements for data processing, cost of survey, main findings etc. in respect of surveys reported by various governmental and non-governmental agencies in the country. This report enables the organisations engaged in sample survey work to share the experience/

expertise in the field of sample surveys. During the year, 47th Annual Report, 1996 (English version) and 48th Annual Report, 1997 (English version) have been released. Hindi version of the 46th Annual Report, 1995 was also released.

Environment statistics

Environment Statistics is a newly emerging area of importance and there is an increasing emphasis on making available relevant data required in the context of promoting environmentally acceptable production technology, conservation of resources, waste minimising, control of pollution of air, water and atmosphere, protection of forests, flora and fauna etc. The environment Statistics Unit continues to close liaison with different organisations dealing with respective subjects including Ministry of Environment and Forests.

The Compendium of Environment Statistics 1997 was brought out by Central Statistical Organisation. The Compendium was widely circulated. The various data source agencies have been requested to supply the data for the Compendium of Environment Statistics, 1998. The draft manuscript is under preparation.

The Central Statistical Organisation has supplied the data on questionnaire on Environmental indicators to the United Nations Statistics Division.

The agenda paper on Development of Environment Statistics was prepared for the meeting of the National Advisory Board on Statistics (NABS).

A two days' National workshop on environment statistics was held at Goa from 12 to 13 January, 1998. The proceedings of the workshop have been brought out in the form of a book which contains various chapters based on the technical sessions held during the workshop. These are Environment Statistics, environment, Population and human health; Status of data bases on Biodiversity, different types of pollution, Human settlements and their impact on environment; Land and soil and their degradation; and Natural Resource Accounting and Recommendation of workshop.

Natural Resource Accounting

The valuation of natural resources has assumed significance under the Agenda 21 of the United Nations Conference on Environment and Development held during June 1992 in Rio de Janeiro. This requires integration of national accounts with natural resource accounting for taking suitable decisions for sustainable development and computing Green GDP. Keeping this in view, the Department of Statistics proposed to launch a pilot project on natural resource accounting in Goa. For this purpose, a Technical Working Group was constituted under the chairmanship of Secretary, Department of Statistics to give guidelines for implementation of the project. On the recommendations of this working group, a background paper was prepared by the Tata Energy Research Institute, assessing the availability of data, need for collection of fresh data and methodology to be followed for the implementation of the project. The second meeting of the Working Group was held on 23 September 1998 in which further task of designing the project in two phases has been entrusted to TERI, to be implemented under the supervision and coordination of Director of Econormics and Statistics, Govt. of Goa. The project will be implemented in two phases with total duration being two and a half years out of which the first phase will include about six months.

Research studies/sample surveys funded

The Department is operating a scheme on "Payment of

Professional services in respect of research studies/ sample surveys and related activities" to generate official statistics, develop methodologies for collection, analysis and processing of data and other research studies on the subjects related to Department of Statistics. About 100 research proposals had been received in response to the advertisement issued in October 97 and these are regularly screened by the Standing Research Advisory Committee set up for the purpose. The following research studies have been approved for funding during the year.

i. Economic liberalisation and labour market flexibility in India.

ii. Informal Sector perspectives in development.

iii. A survey on the gender issues affecting females in household industries in one district of Tamil Nadu.

iv. Development of statistics in the environmental sector.

v. Multi-dimensional problems of women in Kashmir valley.

vi. Shifting pattern of the household consumption of energy in urban area of Orissa.

vii. Role of women in rural economy of India.

viii. Informal sector activities in rural areas : A methodological study.

Price Statistics

The CSO has been compiling and publishing, on a monthly basis, Consumer Price Index for Urban Non-Manual Employees [CPI (UNME)] since 1960. The data on retail prices of goods and services in the consumption basket, used for compilation of CPI(UNME), are collected by the Field Operations Division (FOD) of the National

Sample Survey Organisation (NSSO). The number of goods and services for which data are collected varies from centre to centre. The smallest number is 146 in the case of Imphal; and the largest 345 for Delhi. Data on house rent and off-take of selected commodities are also collected. Based on these data, the CSO compiles and releases the CPI(UNME) on base 1984-85=100. This index is widely used by various agencies for varied purposes, including as an input to the wage and salary adjustment process; indexation of pension and superannuation payments, government taxes, charges and contracts; and as a general measure of inflation. During 1998-99, monthly indices relating to March 1998 to December 1998 have been released upto January 1999. Indices for the months of January-February 1999 are expected to be released between February 1999 and March 1999. Two brochures, giving CPI(UNME) at group and sub-group levels for 59 urban centres and all-India, for the periods July-December 1997 and January-June 1998 respectively, were also released. The brochure for the period July-December 1998 is likely to be released by March 1999.

The all-India general and group level, CPI (UNME) for the period January 1996 to June 1998 is given in the Table on next page. The trends delineated by the movements of all-India CPI(UNME) series at group level, are shown in Chart V.

All-India general and group level CPI(UNME): January 1996 to June 1998

Year	Month	Group 1	Group 2	Group 3	Group 4	Group 5	General
1996	Jan	280	216	227	290	253	262
	Feb	280	217	227	292	254	263
	Mar	283	217	227	294	255	264
	Apr	288	219	227	296	257	267

	May	294	220	227	298	258	271
	Jun	301	220	227	299	259	274
	Jul	306	234	234	300	268	281
	Aug	308	236	235	301	272	283
	Sep	309	239	235	303	274	284
	Oct	311	240	235	305	276	286
	Nov	313	241	235	308	278	288
	Dec	315	242	235	310	279	289
1997	Jan	313	244	243	310	282	290
	Feb	313	246	243	313	284	291
	Mar	313	247	243	314	285	291
	Apr	315	251	243	315	287	293
	May	315	252	243	316	288	293
	Jun	317	252	243	318	290	295
	Jul	319	254	248	319	292	297
	Aug	321	255	248	321	294	299
	Sep	322	264	248	323	298	301
	Oct	324	266	248	325	300	303
	Nov	323	266	248	327	301	303
	Dec	330	268	248	328	304	307
1998	Jan	340	269	255	330	305	313
	Feb	338	270	255	331	306	313
	Mar	335	270	255	332	311 312	
	Apr	341	271	255	333	312	316
	May	348	271	256	335	314	320
	Jun	361	269	256	335	317	326

Presently, the coverage and applicability of the four Consumer Price Indices (CPIs) compiled at national level in the country, namely CPI(IW), CPI(AL), CPI(RL) and CPI(UNME), are restricted to specific segment of the population, as per the respective nomenclatures. As such, a need is felt to develop broad based CPIs which would measure the price behavior and effect of price fluctuation of different commodities and services on the living standards of urban and rural segments of the population of the country. Accordingly, a plan scheme for 'Development of CPI series, separately for urban and rural population at national level' was proposed during Ninth Five Year Plan (1997-2002). In this context, a number of technical issues like consistency of various indices, avoidance of duplication of national efforts, weighting pattern for various items/groups in the series and the target population, are still under the process of inter-ministerial consultations. As the issues related to the subject were quite involved, it has been decided that the Planning Commission would look into the matter in its entirety before further action in this direction is initiated.

Economic Census & Surveys

A scheme of Economic Census and Surveys was initiated in the Department in 1976 to fill the data gaps in the unorganised segments of economy, Accordingly, the first nationwide Economic Census was conducted by the CSO in collaboration with the Directorates of Economics & Statistics in the States/UTs during the last quarter of 1977 which included in its scope and coverage all establishments (enterprises employing at least one hired worker on a fairly regular basis) in the non-agricultural sector only. The second and the third Economic Censuses were synchronised with the house-listing operations of population census and were conducted in 1980 and 1990 respectively. The second and third Economic Censuses had within its scope and coverage all enterprises (establishments as well as own account enterprises) in the entire economy excluding crop production and plantation.

The conduct of fourth Economic Census was approved by the Government at a total cost of Rs.55.93 crores during the period 1997-2000 of the Ninth Five Year Plan with the following objectives:

i. To prepare a sound sampling frame for sample selection it, follow-up surveys

ii. To fill up data gaps in the unorganised sector and to meet the requirements of various data users; and

iii. To assess the impact of liberalisation of entrepreneurial activity.

The fieldwork of the Census was scheduled to be undertaken during 1997-98 itself but in view of the 12th Lok Sabha elections, the activity was slightly delayed and was taken up in 1998-99. Accordingly, the field work has since been completed in all the States/UTs except Andhra Pradesh. Provisional results based on manual tabulation have been received from all except Andhra Pradesh, Assam, Karnataka, Maharashtra, Sikkim, Tamil Nadu, Uttar Pradesh, West Bengal and Andaman & Nicobar Islands. These are under examination. The scrutiny of data collected in the field and coding of schedules for detailed tabulation is in progress. It is proposed to first bring out salient results in respect of key parameters in respect of different States/UTs. A Monitoring Committee at all-India level has been constituted under the chairmanship of Prof J. Roy, Research Professor, Emeritus, ISI, Calcutta to monitor the progress of pre-field operations, field operations, work of data processing and to assess the extent of non-sampling errors based on the findings of post-enumeration check so as to finalise detailed results of Economic Census. The meetings of the Monitoring Committee were held on

18.3.98, 16-17 July 1998 and 21.8.98. The post-enumeration check of the fourth Economic Census has so far been conducted in 21 States/UTs and are likely to be completed in the remaining States/UTs shortly.

Expert Group on definition of Informal Sector

Meeting of the Expert Group formed on the recommendations of NABS under the chairmanship of Prof. S. Tendulkar was held on 5.11.98. The Expert Group has since submitted its report to NABS.

Expert Group on Informal Sector Statistics "Delhi Group"

The Working Group on "International Statistical Programme and Co-ordination" in its meeting held during 1996, had endorsed a proposal of the Expert Group on Economic Statistics for the constitution of various "Voorburg" type groups with a view to addressing critical issues in Economic Statistics. Since, Informal Sector has been growing at a significant pace in most developing countries and India has accumulated some experience in developing a data base, the Department of Statistics, Government of India took initiative to constitute an Expert Group on Informal Sector Statistics christened as 'Delhi Group'.

The second meeting of the Expert Group on Informal Sector Statistics (Delhi Group) was held at Ankara, Turkey during 28-30 April, 1998. Dr. Omer L Bebizlioglu, President of State Institute of Statistics, Ankara, Turkey welcomed the delegates from different countries. Shri M.D. Asthana, Secretary, Department of Statistics gave an opening address as a chair-Person of Delhi Group. The meeting was attended by 37 participants from 9 countries, 5 International Organisations, and other national and international institutions of repute. Discussions during the meeting mainly focussed on current status of data on informal sector and its limitations, country profile, definition of informal sector, survey design, problems in collection of data and quality aspects, contribution of informal sector in terms of employment, value addition, capital formation etc. in the national economy and social security of the workers in informal and unorganised sector. Pursuant to the recommendations of the second meeting, the work on following projects is in progress:

i. Current stocktaking existing country practices and conducting of periodic inventories in future years, including measures of employment and GDP by industry sector and gender statistics (where available).

ii. Clarifying and operationalising the SNA international definition for national accounts and international comparison purpose.

iii. Developing strategies to address Sample frame and weighting issues.

iv. Investigation of quality assurance methods for non-sampling areas (e.g. post enumeration studies).

v. Investigating and developing an appropriate methodology to develop more accurate measures of value added.

Enterprise Surveys

In the Enterprise Survey 1992-93, two sectors viz. Mining & Quarrying and Storage & Warehousing were covered and reports on both the sectors have been released.

(1) Sample Coverage

a. Mining and Quarrying:- A total of 20537 sample enterprises were netted comprising 19740 enterprises from rural areas and 797 from urban areas.

b. Storage & warehousing:- A total of 2156 sample enterprises were netted comprising 1027 enterprises from rural areas and 1129 from urban areas.

(ii) Subject Coverage

(a) Mining and Quarrying—The activity of Mining & Quarrying covers underground and surface mines, quarries and wells, extraction of minerals and all the supplemental activities such as dressing and benefication of ores and other crude materials. These supplemental activities are crushing, screening, Washing, cleaning, grading, milling, melting, palletising, topping and other preparations carried out at mine site which are needed to render the material marketable.

(b) Storage and Warehousing—The activities covered under Storage & Warehousing services sector were warehousing of agricultural products without refrigeration (NIC-740), warehousing of agricultural products with refrigeration-cold storage (NIC-741) and other storage warehousing services (NIC 749).

The following tables provide the key results of the survey: -

A. Mining & Quarrying

Type of enterprise	Estimated Enterprises(No.)	Estimated Workers (No.)	Estimated G.V.A. (Rs. in lakhs)
Own Account enterprises	133138	324108	9379
Non-Directory Establishment	46498	166343	7941
Directory Establishment	55490	1015850	56779
Total	235126	1506301	74099

B. Storage & Warehousing

Type of enterprise	Estimated Enterpfises(No.)	Estimated Workers (No.)	Estimated G.V.A. (Rs. in Iakhs)
Own Account enterprises	29311	40865	5153
Non-Directory Establishment	31617	88675	29951
Directory Establishment	7179	68305	27605
Total	68107	197845	62709

Training

The Training Division of the Central Statistical Organisation (CSO) organises regular training courses for the officers of the Indian Statistical Service (ISS) and statistical personnel of the Central and State Governments and Public Sector Undertakings. Besides, the Division also organises specialised training courses for the officers of the ISS and those sponsored by some international Organisations.

During the year, Eleven training programmes of varied duration from one week courses to 8 week courses and one year programme for various senior/middle level officers, students, statistical personnel and direct recruits to Grade IV of Indian Statistical Service have been organised. Subjects covered are modules on Official Statistics, Management Techniques, Construction of Life Tables and Population Projections, Planning and Evaluation, Theory of Samples Surveys, Time Series and Forecasting, Organisation of Sample Surveys, Survey Design and training programme on Financial and Banking Statistics, National and International Statistical Systern and National Accounts Statistics. The division has also conducted seven Seminar Talks on varied subjects.

Statistical Intelligence Unit

The Statistical Intelligence Unit, Central Statistical Organisation is continuously engaged in collection, compilation and updation of various socio economic data series and their trends in respect of India for dissemination to the national as well as international agencies including UN/ESCAP. Besides this, the Unit has also been entrusted with the job of implementing the plan scheme on awards and fellowships for outstanding and meritorious research work in statistics under the Ninth Five Year Plan.

4

National Sample Survey Organisation

The National Sample Survey Organisation (NSSO) carries out socio-economic surveys, undertakes field work for the Annual Survey of Industries and follow-up surveys of Economic Census, sample checks on area enumeration and crop estimation surveys and prepares the urban frames useful in drawing of urban samples, besides collection of price data from rural and urban sectors. This organisation, functions under the overall direction of a Governing Council with requisite independence and autonomy in the matter of collection, processing and publication of NSS data. In addition to the non- official Chairman, the Governing Council is composed of five academicians, five data users from Central and State Government departments and senior officers of the Department.

The NSSO is headed by the Director General and Chief Executive Officer (DG&CEO) who is responsible for co-ordinating and supervising all activities of the oiganisation and is assisted by a small secretariat called Co-ordination and Publication Division (CPD). The DG&CEO is also M ember- Secretary of the Governing Council. The major activities of the NSSO pertains to Survey Design, Field Operations, Processing of data collected and releasing of the results based on survey.

The Survey Design and Research Division and Data Processing Division have its headquarters at Calcutta. The Field Operations Division has its headquarters at Delhi and Faridabad with a network of six Zonal offices spread throughout the country. The Data Processing Division with its headquarters at Calcutta has Data Processing Centres at Delhi, Giridih, Nagpur, Bangalore, Ahmedabad and Calcutta.

Governing Council of NSSO

During the year 1998-99, two (70th and 71st) meetings of the Governing Council of NSSO were held in April and July 98 respectively. In the 70th meeting the sample design and schedules of enquiry of 55th round of NSS were discussed and finalised. The meeting also considered the proposal of Ministry of Welfare for undertaking survey of street children available in the country. After lot of discussion, it was decided not to take up the survey immediately as the launching of same would primarily call for a change in the methodology of sample selection in addition to the change in the method of collection of data.

However, it was suggested that if a separate listing of houseless households/houseless children through schedules 0.2 of 55th round is made, the same could perhaps throw some light on the proportion of such cases. In the 71st meeting, undertaking of Special Survey for Generating Alternative Estimates of Value Added Per Worker, at the behest of National Accounts Division (NAD), of CSO, was discussed and it was decided that the proposed survey be undertaken as an exploratory study without terming it as a NSS roudd. The special survey started on 17th August, 1998 and will continue up to June 99. The 55th round survey on Consumer Expenditure and Employment will, as a result, commence from July 1999 - June 2000.

Workshops for processing of NSS 54th round were organised at Calcutta during April, 21-22,1998, Ahmedabad on 27. 4. 1998 and Nagpur on 11.5.1998.

Two meetings of the 'Expert Committee to examine wide variation in the data sets on the same subject' were held at Mahalanobis Bhavan, Calcutta on 1.5.1998 and 21.9.98.

Working Group meeting on the Tabulation Plan for NSS 54th round was held at Calcutta under the Chairmanship of Prof. Pravin Visaria, Chairman, Governing Council, NSSO.

Conferences on Special Survey on Non-agricultural enterprises were organised at Jaipur, Bangalore and Guwahati on 4.8 98, 9.8.98 and 24.8.98 respectively.

Workshop on Multipliers and Estimation Procedure for NSS Surveys and Special Survey on value added per worker was held at Mahalanobis Bhavan, Calcutta on 4.8.98 and 9.8.98.

Statistical co-ordination

The role of NSSO in the field of Agricultural Statistics is to provide technical guidance to the States in the conduct of Crop Estimation Surveys aimed for objective estimation of yield of principal crops. The main objective of the scheme is to locate through Joint efforts of Central and State agencies, deficiencies in the system of collection of Crop Statistics in each State/Union Territory and to suggest remedial measures, Under the scheme, sample checks on the primary field work relating to area enumeration in approximately, 5000 villages and supervision of 15,000 crop cutting experiments are undertaken in every agricultural year.

In addition to this sample check on aggregation of area figures above the village level i.e. at Tehsil, District and State level is also undertaken in 13 land record States spread over 32 Regions of NSSO as a pan of Improvement of Crop Statistics (ICS) programme since 1980-81.

During the agricultural year 1997-98 up to December' 98 the work relating to sample check on area enumeration was carried out in 1270,, 4949, 4649 and 3969 villages as against 1270, 4949, 4649 and 4029 villages planned during Early Kharif, Rabi and Summer seasons respectively. Likewise 15648 crop cutting experiments were supervised as against 15660 experiments planned.

For agricultural year 1998-99, checking of area enumeration was completed in 1269 villages during Early Kharif 4434 villages during Kharif and 8 villages during Rabi season up to December 1998 as against 1270, 4949 and 4649 planned respectively. For sample check on crop cutting experiments 1170, 7080 and 10 experiments were supervised up to December 1998 during Early Kharif, Kharif and Rabi respectively as against 1262, 8956 and 4646 -37- experiments planned. By March 1999, another 92, 1652 and 1028 crop cutting experiments during Early Kharif, Kharif and Rabi respectively are expected to be supervised.

The data collected through the supervision of crop cutting experiments at harvest stage are also utilised to compute the advance estimates of yield rates of specified crops of the states covered. For the agricultural year 1997-98 as many as 167 estimates of yield rates have been forwarded to Ministry of Agriculture, New Delhi as per the pre-decided time schedule. 47 advance estimates of yield rates spread over various crops and States for the year 1998-99 have also been issued by December 1998.

The findings of ICS are brought out in the form of Reports on the Status of Estimation of Crop Production in States as well as in all India. The State wise Reports are brought out during each agricultural year. A consolidated report on all India Status is also prepared annually. During the year under reference, the Statewise reports for the year 1996-97 for Kharif and Rabi have been issued for all the States, The All India Report on Status of Estimation of crop production in India 1995-96 have also been issued and the draft report for 1996-97 have been prepared.

Another report based on Crop Estimation Survey titled "Consolidated Results of Crop Estimation Surveys (CES)" on Principal Crops in India for the year 1995-96 has also been brought out during the year.

High Level Co-ordination Committees (HLCCs) have been formed in the States to deliberate, discuss and sort out organisational & operational issues pertaining to various aspects of Agricultural Statistics. They provide a link for proper co-ordination between the centre and states forming a basis for the improvement of quality and timeliness of Agricultural Statistics- During the year under report, meetings of High Level Co- ordination committees were held in the States of Rajasthan, Punjab, Bihar, Kerala, Madhya Pradesh, Karnataka and West Bengal.

In addition to High Level Co-ordination Committees, district Level Committees are also functioning at decentralised level. These committees are entrusted with the task of examining, at the field level, reasons of variations in the entries as recorded by the Patwaries and as observed by Central/State Supervisors during sample check on area enumeration under ICS. The functioning of committees goes a long way in affecting improvement in the State system of area and yield statistics. Response in this case during the year has also been quite encouraging.

Outside the purview of mandated association of NSSO in Improvement of Crop Statistics, the Field Operations Division has taken up a very important task of updation of Crop Calendar for the country at the behest of the Secretary, Department of Statistics as the present Crop Calendar is more than 30 years old. The first phase of updation of Crop Calendar on the basis of information received from the states has been completed. The updated calendar gives information relating to periods of sowing, harvesting and marketing for 38-different crops in the States. It is due to initiatives and efforts of the NSSO (FOD) that Crop calendar has been updated after a lapse of more than 30 years since its last version of 1967.

The NSSO regularly collects retail rural price data on monthly basis from shops/outlets in selected markets located in a sample of 419 villages in respect of 129 selected essential items (in old series) and from another non-overlapping set of 603 villages for 260 items (revised series) for compilation of Consumer Price Index number for Agricultural Labourers by the labour Bureau. These index numbers are published in the monthly publication 'Indian Labour Journal' of the Labour Bureau, the latest (November 1998) issue of which give the index for the month of July 1998. Commodity-wise average rural retail prices as per the old series arc continued to be published in the Monthly Abstract of Statistics (MAS) The latest September 1998 issue gives the average prices for the month of March 1998.

Survey on land & livestock holdings and debt & investment

The NSS 48th round (January - December, 1992) was devoted to the survey on Land & Livestock holdings and Debt & Investment besides the usual enquiry oil consumer expenditure. Based oil the survey results of Debt & Investment, seven reports have been released.

Survey on Housing condition and Migration with special emphasis on Slum dwellers

In the 49th round (January - June, 1993) of NSS, Information on Housing condition and Migration with special emphasis on Slum dwellers besides the enquiry on consumer expenditure was collected. One report on 'Migration in India' has been released on the basis of survey results.

Quinquennial survey on household consumer expenditure and employment & unemployment

The Fifth quinquennial survey on household consumer expenditure and employment & unemployment was carried-out in the 50th round (July, 1993- June, 1994) of NSS- During the year, one report on 'Employment and Unemployment situation among religious groups III India' has been released.

Survey on unorganised manufacturing sector

The NSS 51st round (July, 1994 - June, 1995) was devoted to the survey on unorganised manufacturing and repairing enterprises/establishments besides the regular enquiry on consumer expenditure. On the basis of survey results, one report on consumer expenditure and three reports on unorganised manufacturing enterprises have been released.

Survey on health care and participation in education

NSS 52nd round (July, 1995 - June, 1996) was devoted to social consumption with focus on morbidity, health care, education and problems of aged persons besides the regular enquiry on consumer expenditure. Till date, one report on 'Consumer expenditure' and one report each on Participation in education, Morbidity, Child Care and Aged Persons have been released on the basis of the survey results during the year.

Survey on trade

The survey on unorganised trade covering the Own-account trading enterprises and Non-directory trading establishments in addition to the usual consumer expenditure was carried-out in the 53rd round (January - December, 1997) of NSS. One report on consumer expenditure has been released so far and two draft reports on small trading units in India have also been released.

Annual survey on consumer expenditure

To maintain continuity, data on household consumer expenditure, employment and unemployment are being collected in every NSS round, through relatively small sample besides regular quinquennial surveys. The field work of such surveys in respect of NSS 54th round (January - June, 1998) is completed. On the basis of the survey results, one draft report on household expenditure and employment situation in India will be prepared during the year.

Survey on common property resources, village facilities, sanitation & hygiene and services

NSS 54th round (January - June, 1998) was devoted to the Survey on Common Property Resources, Village Facilities, Sanitation & Hygiene and Services. During the year, three draft reports will be prepared on the basis of the survey results.

Urban frame survey

For conducting socio-economic enquiries in urban area an updated frame of sampling units is an essential prerequisite and Urban Frame Survey is being carried out by Field Operations Division to meet this objective. To ensure this, the frame is being updated on a regular basis once in five years. For the first time UFS Blocks were used for enumeration of Enterprises in Economic Census

1998. Unique identification codes were assigned to each urban block of Urban Frame 1992-97 for the purpose which led to computerisation of the details pertaining to more than 3.5 lakh blocks in the frame. These blocks are demarcated in about 15,000 maps called Investigator Units Maps (IV Units Maps) to facilitate easy identification.

Field work of the 6th phase (1997-2002) of the Urban Frame Survey, which commenced from July' 97 is currently in progress and till December 1998, work in respect of 82913 blocks have been completed /updated in 624 -40- towns as against an estimated target of 3.6 lakh blocks in about 4675 towns comprising urban agglomerations and their constituent towns. During the remaining period of 1998-99 another 18000 UFS blocks are expected to be completed/updated.

The survey being unique in nature and the records and maps being of significant importance in organising and conducting enquiries in urban sector, a programme of commercialisation of maps and other records was initiated in the year 1988. Up to December 1998 an amount of Rs. 8,30,800 has been realised on this account.

Enterprise survey

As a part of the programme of organising follow up surveys of Economic Census, large scale enterprise surveys on selected sectors of national economy are conducted with the objectives to collect detailed information on inventory of fixed assets, outstanding loans etc. in respect of enterprises in such sectors.

Annual survey of industries

Field work for Annual Survey of Industries (ASI) is carried out by the Field Operations Division (FOD), NSSO. In the ASI 1996-97, which was concluded in June 1998, the over all completion was 70,279 factories as against the net allotment of 73,598 factories, the percentage rate being 95.5 % Field work for ASI 97-98: Substantial changes in the sample design have been incorporated on the basis of the recommendations of the "Technical Group for revision of sampling design of annual survey of Industries" with reduced sample size and only two compacted categories - (A) Census Sector, which covers - (1) all industrial units of the 12 less industrially developed States/UTs, (ii) Industrial units having 200 or more workers, (iii) All Electric Undertakings and PSUs and significant Industries having input/output/GVA/NVA as per ASI 93-94, ASI 94-95 & ASI 95-96, supplied by CSO (IS Wing), Calcutta and (B) Sample Sector - which covers the entire ASI frame minus the industrial units of (A) census sector.

Another salient feature is the introduction of the shorter and user friendly schedule with the innovative questions in the Part - I of ASI schedule designed to fetch, inter-alia, information on - (a) Quality Assurance, (b) Information Technology, (c) International Trade, (d) Capacity Utilisation of plant and machinery, (e) proprietorship of product/by product and (f) Pollution.

The field work for ASI 97-98 was taken up in September 1998 after issue of notices and targeted to complete the whole work in record time by November 1998. The overall completion is 33,308 factories out of a net allotment of 34,890 factories (95.5%) up to December 1998.

Plan schemes

Keeping in view the modernisation of activities to be carried out, two Plan Schemes under the names (1) Organisation of Library and Modernisation of Statistical System, and (il) Post Survey Evaluation of sample surveys are being implemented in SDRD.

The following three schemes are being implemented in Data Processing Division during Ninth Plan:

(a) Construction of office building for NSSO at Calcutta.

(b) Rationalisation of Data Processing Facilities and Upgradation of the existing Micro Processing System for accelerating data processing and creation of data base for socio-economic Surveys.-

The following plan schemes are being implemented in Field Operation Division, NSSO during Ninth Plan:

(i) Construction/Purchase of office accommodation for field offices.

(ii) Strengthening and streamlining of field offices.

(iii) Strengthening of training facilities at Zonal Centres and

(iv) On line transmission of Survey data from field offices to processing centres and modernisation in the data collection system.

The following two schemes are being implemented in Co-ordination and Publication Division (CPD) of NSSO during Ninth Plan:

(i) Grant-in-aid to northeastern States of Manipur, Tripura, Mizoram and Arunachal Pradesh for carrying out Central NSS work.

(ii) Strengthening and modernisation of NSS Publication Wing,

Training

FOD

The 6 Zonal Training Centres of NSSO continued their activities of imparting in-service training to the technical staff of FOD. During the year 277 trainees at the levels of Superintendents, Assistant Superintendents, Investigators, UDCs and LDCs were imparted training in 8 batches in Operator Level Course (OLC) at Bangalore and Nagpur.

During December' 98, "Specialised Training Programmes" of 6 days durations were held in all the Zonal centres and AS Wing, Faridabad. In all, 130 Investigators and 149 Assistant Superintendents participated in the training.

The special training for Superintendents was held from 22.1.99 to 29.1.99. The broad topics covered were-National Statistical System, Modernisation and Computerisation of NSS, Computer appreciation module covering data collection, transmission and processing of data, Human Resource Development covering Motivation, Leadership 'and Management and the surveys conducted by Field Operations Division. This includes Annual Survey of Industries, Agricultural Statistics, Socio-Economic Statistics, Price Collection, Urban Frame Survey, etc. and field visits followed by a feed back -42- NSSO/CSO session.

The objective is to expose all the field staff to this programme during 1998-99 and 1999-2000. Eight such programmes are proposed to be organised in each of the six zonal centres and Faridabad.

In addition to above training programmes organised by the Division, its officers served as faculty in various training programmes organised by the Training Division from time to time. Staff of the Division also participated in training programmes organised by the organisations like Training Division, Central Statistical Organisation, Institute of Secretariat Training and Management and National Informatics Centre.

A special training programme was arranged for XXII Batch of the ISS probationers during the months of September-October 98. This included two- day orientation programme at FOD Headquarters and attachment of the probationers to different zonal Centres for detailed exposure to various schemes undertaken by the Division. They were also engaged in actual data collection in the field in a survey on Sex Ratio in the state of Haryana.

S/Shri M. Neelakanthan, Deputy Director General, Dr. A.K. Yogi, Director (North Zone), K.L. Taneja, J.P. Misra and S.N. Singh, Joint Directors participated in the workshop on Modernisation of Indian Statistical System during 14-16 September' 98 at Vigyan Bhavan, New Delhi as part of negotiation of World Bank Aid. They worked as co-ordinator/reporters in the different working groups in the workshop constituted to deliberate on sector specific issues.

The training workshop organised annually to discuss procedures to be adopted for processing data of a particular survey round, provides an opportunity for an exchange of ideas and fruitful interaction amongst the participants- Besides the staff and officers of DPD; representatives from State Statistical Bureaus also participate in the training-workshop. The D.P.Centre-wise training workshop for the 54th round devoted to inquiry on Common Property Resources, Sanitation and Hygiene (Schedule 3 1), Common Property Resources and Village facilities (Schedule 3.3) as well as Consumer expenditure (schedule 1.0) were organised between April and May '98. In- house training on Department of Statistics and WINDOWS had been organised in the DPD for benefit of the officers of both DPD & SDRD.

Dissemination and Publication

The results of the National Sample Surveys are published in the quarterly journal of the Department 'Sarvekshana'.

List of publications and the reports released by the NSSO during 1998-99.

Computer centre

The Government of India, with distant foresight, visualised the urgency and necessity of Introducing the Computerisation in the official work during mid -sixties. Consequently, it was decided during 1967, to set up this Computer Centre as an attached office tinder Deptt. of Statistics, Cabinet Secretariat, to cater to the Data Processing needs of this Department and other Government Offices under different Ministries. With the clear objectives of creating Computer awareness, this Centre right from its inception, continued to perform pioneering tasks of building Data Processing Institutions in various organisations of the Government of India, by imparting intensive training In Systems Analysis, Data Processing and by providing consonancy and Support Services in the fields of Electronic Data Processing (EDP).

Although, over a period of time, the Deptt. of Statistics was placed under the Ministry of Planning, but its data processing applications kept on increasing rapidly. This Centre, as one of its major tasks, undertook the processing Of voluminous data running into several million records, collected by the National Sample Survey Organisation (NSSO) through various Socio- Economic Surveys, follow-tip Surveys of Economic Census and Annual Surveys of Industries conducted periodically by the NSSO and CSO.

It also provides, where possible, computing service and facilities to other Government Departments and Organisations including State Governments.

On a regular basis, a number of training courses on Electronic Data Processing are conducted for different levels of officers belonging to Indian Statistical Service

(ISS) namely, EDP Training to participants of Junior Certificate Course in Statistics (JCCS), Direct Recruits to Grade IV of ISS, Training on Software Packages to Senior/Middle level ISS officers etc. This Centre had also earlier conducted training courses on Electronic Data Processing for Internationally sponsored trainees tinder different United Nations Development Programmes (UNDP), as decided by the Deptt. of Statistics. As per the organisational set up, this Centre is headed by Executive Director (an SAG level officer of ISS) recently redesignated as Deputy Director General, who is assisted by one Additional Director, 4 Joint Directors and 13 Deputy Directors and a team of 30 officers, besides 124 technical and administrative staff in day-to-day functioning of this centre.

Evolution of computer system

The Centre initially started functioning with three Honeywell-400 second generation refurbished computer systems in 1967 as one of the major Computer Centre in the Govt. of India. In 1981, a more powerful third generation Burroughs-3845 computer system having inter alia, on-line program development and data entry facilities, as part of its configuration was installed in replacement of three Honeywell-400 Computer Systems. On account of technological advancements in the Computer industry, the Burroughs-3845 computer system was replaced by a more modem (4th generation) and powerful mainframe computer system DPS-7000/240 in May, 1992. This computer system has more capacity and capabilities for simultaneously handling of varied nature of applications as compared to earlier computer systems. The present mainframe Computer System runs on two-shifts basis having about 90.30% uptime as compared to the total scheduled time till December, 98.

Approach towards modernisation of data preservation

The basic data processed at this Centre pertaining to Socio-Economic Surveys, Prices and Industries etc. have been preserved in Magnetic Tapes, the only appropriate storage magnetic media available for this purpose till early nineties. Experiencing obvious inconveniences in maintaining the large number of such tapes, steps had been taken to transfer the data onto compact discs (CD). Accordingly, the Centre has procured two Pentium PCs with CD- ROM READER and WRITER facilities for preservation of data on CD-ROM and thus releasing the magnetic tapes for reuse in other Computer applications. The other two Pentium-based PCs (without CD preparation facilities) are being used for data processing and application development work.

Main activities

The Centre discharges the following main activities: -

i) Data Preparation

ii) Building of Data Processing System comprising of -

(a) Systems Analysis and Design

(b) Development of Software

(c) Computer operation, processing of Data and production of final results.

(d) Documentation of the Computerised System for current and subsequent references and use.

iii) Training on Electronic Data Processing Activities for ISS Officers.

iv) Preservation of data and results on computer media for subsequent use and dissemination.

Data preparation

The centre is essentially responsible for processing of data made available to it on magnetic tapes as inputs, which is transferred to Computer hard disc media before processing on mainframe computer system. For data entry, the centre has been using PC-based electronic computers. However, towards the end of 1994, 32 PC-386 based machines were also purchased to modernise the Data Entry Unit and to supplement the data entry resources.

During the period from April, 1998 to December, 1998, about 18.39 lakhs records were keyed/verified through these data entry machines. For Enterprise Survey 1993-94 and 1995-96, this centre also provided assistance in pre-data entry coding and examination of the coverage listings for checking the missing schedules.

The centre is however, also responsible for data preparation (i.e., keying in the data through data entry machines) relating to:

(i) Consumer Price Indices for Urban Non-Manual Employees CPI (UNME) - Monthly returns.

(ii) Enterprise Survey - 1993-94:- Sch. 2.31, 2.33 and 2.42 Transport Sector and Hotels & Restaurants.

(iii) Enterprise Survey 1995-9&- Sch. 2.41 Directory of Trading Enterprises.

Program development and computing activities

The targets for different stages of data processing of various projects assigned to the Computer Centre were, as usual, set at the beginning of the year, as a part of the Annual Action Plan 1998-99. The progress on the achievements of each of the projects was regularly reviewed quarterly by the Secretary, Department of Statistics.

Jobs completed during the period from April '98 to Dec. '98

(i) Consumer price indices for urban non-manual employees (CPI, UNME). (1984-85=100):- Indices up to November 1998 were generated.

(ii) Enterprise survey 1992-93 Sch. 2.34:- Storage and Warehousing: Revised final tables were generated.

(iii) Fourth economic census 98:- This Centre has produced a PC-based Data Processing Package for Data Entry, Validation of data files, Updation and Auto-Correction of data files in the first stage. And in the second stage a Tabulation Package for generating the Summary Statements for preparing the sampling frames for follow up surveys of Economic Census, main tables and special tables for facilitating the analysis and report writing work. The use of the first Data Processing Package was demonstrated to the representatives of different States/UTs during a Workshop conducted in July, 1998.

(iv) Enterprise surveys 1993-94:-

(a) Transport Sch. 2.31, 2.32 AND 2-33 Data entry and coverage checking of the data entrusted to Computer Centre completed alongwith the computation of multipliers.

(b) Sch 2.42 hotels and restaurants: Data Entry, coverage checking, and validation of data completed alongwith the development of software for tabulation. The trial tables for two sample states were also produced for examination of the ECD, CSO.

(v) Enterprise survey 1995-96:SCH.2.41 directory of trading enterprises:- Development of softwares for printing missing and duplicates error lists, updation of file and computer scrutiny of data files were completed' The generation of first cycle of error lists (content checking) has been completed for all the States/UT's.

(vi) Time use survey:- System Design and Development of Software for processing of data has been initiated. The software for multiplier computation and files creation is expected to be completed during this period.

(vii) National data workhouse of official statistics:- Discussions held with the officers of Labour Bureau, Department of Company Affairs and Department of Education on availability and type of data, its periodicity etc. Similar discussions with other Departments are in progress. Thereafter, a report will be prepared.

(viii) Dissemination of data:-

(a) Annual Survey of Industries.

(i) Census (Summary) data at All-India 3 digit level of NIC for the years 1991-92 to 1994-95 to CSO.

(ii) 1989-90 (Detail) data on input-output items on selected industries to NAD, CSO.

(iii) All-India, Statewise (Summary) data at 2 digit and 3 digit level of NIC to Institute of Human Development.

(iv) Summary data for the years 1993-94 and 1994- 95 to CSO IS Wing.

(v) Summary data at 3 digit level for the years 1984-85 to 1994-95 to Circon Research Consultancy New Delhi.

(b) Consumer price Index (UNME):- Data for the period Jan. 97 to June 98 - to CSO.

(c) National Sample Survey:-

(i) Special tables from data on schedule 1.0 (consumer expenditure), 43rd and 50th round for National Research Centre for Sorghum.

(ii) Religion-wise tables on 43rd and 50th round schedule 1.0 (Consumer Expenditure).

(iii) Generation of weighting diagram for CPI (UNME) from 50th round schedule 1.0 (Consumer Expenditure) data.

(iv). Supply of NSSO data to various users from April to November, 1998 on CDs,

(ix) The data transferred from magnetic tapes to CD-ROMs:-

(a) Annual survey of industries

(1) Detail: Basic data for the year 1978-79.

(2) Summary- Data for the years 1974-75, 1976-77 to 1988-89.

(b) Consumer Price Index (UNME) Monthly data for the months of February 1996 to November 1998 were transferred on CDs.

(c) Directory Manufacturing Establishments 78-79 (partly).

(d) Directory Manufacturing Establishments 84-85.

(e) Directory Trading Enterprises 90-91.

Training activities during the year 1998-99

(a) Courses conducted under the auspices of Department of Statistics:

(i) Training on software packages for ISS Middle level officers: A two week's course from 29.6.97

to 10.7.97 on software packages for 13 Senior and Middle level ISS officers nominated by the Deptt. of Statistics, was organised.

(ii) Junior Certificate Course for Statisticians : A three week's EDP Training Course is scheduled from 8.2-99 to 26.2.99.

(b) Training obtained in India:

(i) Five Officers obtained training on MS-OFFICE 97 for one week from 31st August, 98 to 4th Sept. 98. at CMC Training Centre, New Delhi.

ii) One Officer obtained training on MS-OFFICE 97 at Deptt. of Electronics Training Centre, New Delhi.

5

Indian Statistical Institute

In early thirties, realising the necessity for advancement of theoretical and applied Statistics in India, the Indian Statistical Institute came into being with the pioneering initiative and efforts of Professor P.C. Mahalanobis. The Indian Statistical Institute was registered on 28 April, 1932 as a non-profit distributing learned society under the societies Registration Act 1860. From the beginning, the Institute started showing its excellence in its own way. As the Institute expanded its research, teaching, training and project activities it started earning national/ international recognition. For its Substantial contribution to the quality of theoretical and applied statistical work, the Institute had been recognised as an "Institute of National Importance" by an Act of Parliament, known as "Indian Statistical Institute Act No. 57 of 1959". The Act has conferred on the Institute the fight to hold examinations and award degrees/diplomas in Statistics. Significantly, none other than Pandit Jawaharlal Nehru, the then Prime Minister himself piloted the bill in the Parliament in 1959. As a result degree courses leading to Bachelor of Statistics (B.Stat.) and Master of Statistics (M.Stat.) and post graduate diplomas in SQC & OR and Computer Science were started from June 1960. The Institute was also empowered to award Ph.D./D.Sc. Degree from the same year. Subsequently, Master of Technology courses in Computer Science and in Quality,

Reliability & Operations Research were also started. Scope was further enlarged as the Institute was empowered to award degrees/diplomas in Statistics, Mathematics, Quantitative Economics, Computer Science and such other subjects related to Statistics by virtue of "Indian Statistical Institute (Amendment) Act, 1995, No. 38 of 1995" by the Parliament effective from 18 September, 1995. Recognition of the Institute by Acts of Parliament, gave a greater encouragement to research activities not only in Statistics/ Mathematics but also in various branches of Natural and Social Sciences, Physics and Earth Sciences, Biological Sciences. Statistical Quality Control & Operations Research, Library and Information Sciences in a broader way.

Over the years, the Institute has been playing a key role in the development of statistical theory and methods in promoting research and practical applications in different areas of natural and social sciences. Sankhya - The Indian Journal of Statistics, being published by the Institute since 1933, is still considered as one of the leading Statistical journals of the world. Research in economics was greatly stimulated when in 1954 Prime Minister Jawaharlal Nehru entrusted the preparation of the draft Second Five-Year Plan of the country to Professor Mahalanobis and the Institute. The "Draft" submitted by Professor Mahalanobis and the planning models formulated by him in that connection have since been regarded as major contributions to economic, planning in India. In the field of Computer Science, the Institute has a rich tradition. In 1953, a small analog computer was designed and built in the Institute. In 1956, the Institute acquired a HEC-2M machine from the UK which was the first digital computer in India. In early sixties, the Institute, in collaboration with the Jadavpur University, undertook the design, development and fabrication of a fully transistorised digital computer, called ISIJU- I which was commissioned in 1966 by Shri M.C. Chagla, the then Minister of Education, Government of India. High quality research and development in the field of computer science is being carried out by the internationally acclaimed scientists of the Institute.

The ISI also played a pioneering role in starting the Statistical Quality Control (SQC) movement in India by organising a visit of Professor W.A. Shewhart, the father of SQC, to India in 1948 and later by inviting other experts like W.E. Deming, Genichi Taguchi etc. for the same purpose. SQC promotional work of the Institute then gradually spread all over the industrial centres in India under a comprehensive programme covering education and training, applied research and consultancy services. Considering it's meaningful contributions, over the years, Govt. of India has made ISI a permanent member of "Quality-Council" in August, 1998. With a view to developing innovative methodologies for collection and analysis of quality survey data, interacting and collaborating with organisations like NSSO, CSO, Planning Commission, RBI, etc., promoting the growth of interdisciplinary research in statistics and data analysis in the Institute, and disseminating the methodologies (old and new) to the scientific, academic and research organisations, a Survey Research and Data Analysis Centre (SURDAC) has been established at the Institute in February 1997.

Such a Centre would benefit the planning processes and national development of the country. In 1995, the Plan and policy Research Unit (PPRU) was established under the Planning Unit at Delhi Centre which has already undertaken several projects of national and international importance. Thus, the Institute has been maintaining a very high standard as a centre of excellence and earning national/international recognitions true to its tradition.

To provide funds to the Institute, Govt. of India constitutes a committee each year under section &(I) of the Act to prepare a programme of work agreed to be undertaken by the Institute in the following year.

During the year, the Institute has an irreparable loss at the demise of It's Chairman, Shri P.N. Haksar who passed away for heavenly abode on November 27, 1998. Shri Haksar was the Chairman of the Institute from I November 1973 till his death and rendered valuable service, help and suggestions for continuance of the Institute as an Institute of excellence in the world of Statistics and related areas, with the objective enunciated in the Memorandum of Association of the Institute. Professor M.G.K. Menon and Professor S.B. Rao continued to act as the President and the Director of the Institute respectively during the year,

During the academic session 1998-99, 8164 candidates applied for admission and were called for written/selection tests for the various courses offered by the Institute viz. B.Stat. (Hons.), M.Stat. (Math. and Stat. stream), M.S. in Quantitative Economics, M.Tech. in Computer Science, M.Tech. in Quality, Reliability and Operations Research, Two-year part-time Post- Graduate Diploma in SQC and OR; Research Fellowships in Statistics, Mathematics, Economics, Computer & Communication Sciences, Theoretical Physics, and Applied Mathematics, Anthropology, Geology, Sociology, Biometry, One year part-time courses in Statistical Methods and Applications and the course on Operation and Programming of Automatic Data processing Equipment. Admission tests were conducted at 21 different Centres all over the country. A total of 6260 candidates finally appeared at the admission tests and a total of 527 candidates who qualified in the written tests were called for interview. Based on the performance in the written tests and the interview, 200 candidates were offered admission to various courses during the academic session under review.

Encouraged by the recent amendment of the ISI Act 1995, the Institute started a M.S. Course on Quantitative Economics to meet some of the needs of the country for development of Human Resources and Research. The first batch of this course, MS(QE) graduated in July 1998. The annual examinations for all the regular courses were held in May/June 1998. The 1998-99 academic session commenced on 2 July, 1998. One hundred forty nine candidates received their degrees and diplomas at the Thirtysecond Annual Convocation of the Indian Statistical Institute held on 29 June, 1998. 13 Research Fellows were awarded Ph.D. degree of the Indian Statistical Institute.

Professional examinations in statistics

During the period, the Examination Committee of the Institute conducted professional examinations for the Statistical Assistantship Certificate, Junior Diploma in Statistics and Senior Diploma in Statistics which were held at Bangalore, Calcutta, Delhi, Bombay, Hyderabad, Madras, Lucknow twice in a year usually in the month of April/May and December respectively.

The total number of students who have qualified for award of the Certificates and Diplomas in professional examinations in statistics we 488 and 281 respectively. The Government of India recognised the Junior Diploma in Statistics as equivalent to a Bachelor's degree in Statistics while Senior Diploma in Statistics to a Master's Degree in Statistics.

International Statistical Education Cntre (ISEC)

The ISEC, which was opened in 1950, is operated jointly by the International Statistical Institute and the Indian Statistical Institute, under the auspices of the UNESCO and the Government of India. The Centre as an associated body of the Institute functions under a Joint Board of Directors. The Directors represent International Statistical Institute, Indian Statistical Institute and the Govt. of India. Professor P.C. Mahalanobis was the Chairman of the Board of Directors since its inception in 1950 until his death in 1972. Since then, National Professor C.R. Rao, F.R.S, has been the Chairman of the Board.

The Centre provides training in Theoretical, Applied Statistics at the various levels for selected participants from the countries in the Middle-East, South and South-East Asia, the Far East and the Commonwealth countries in Africa, sponsored by respective Governments. Major training programme of the Centre is a 10-month regular course. In addition, special courses of varying duration are also organised. Since inception, the Centre has provided training to 1250 trainees from 56 countries,

During the year the 10-month regular course (52nd term) commenced on 1st June, 1998 with 16 trainees from Srilanka, Nepal, Maldives, Bhutan, Cambodia, Korea, Myanmar, Uganda and Philippines. One officer from Mangolia has undergone a special training course in Sample Surveys from October, 1998.

Research work

The research activities of the Institute are grouped into the following Divisions : Theoretical Statistics and Mathematics; Applied Statistics; Physics and Earth Sciences; Computer and Communication Sciences-, Biological Sciences-, Social Sciences; Statistical Quality

Control & Operations Research; and Library, Documentation & Information Sciences. In addition, the Computer & Statistical Services Centre (CSSC) has the responsibilities of the management of in-house computer system of the Institute and providing computing and statistical services to scientific workers.

Statistical quality control and operations research

The SQC and OR division set up in 1953, now operates with 10 units located at Bangalore, Baroda, Calcutta (2 Units), Hyderabad, New Delhi, Bombay, Coimbatore, Madras, Pune. During last four decades of its existence, the division provided consultancy on the application of Quality Management system, concepts and tools to over one thousand establishments.

These activities included designing and implementing ISO 9000 quality system to more than 60 organisations leading to certification and training over one million engineers/supervisors and operators in various aspects of quality related topics. Besides these the division organised Indian and International conferences, pioneered large scale application of Design of experiments, conducted professional programmes like M.Tech. (SQC & OR), Post Graduate Diploma in SQC & OR, Part-time certificate course in SQC; carried out Quality Mission Programme aimed at imparting intensive training for trainers in the area of Quality Management application and training in industries and undertaken applied research and advancement of application knowledge and skill.

The SQC movement in India dates back to 1948 when Prof. Walter Shewhert, father of SQC, visited India at the invitation of Prof. P. C. Mahalanobis and conducted a large number of training programmes in industry and top management awareness programmes throughout India. To commemorate the 50th anniversary of the movement, a national conference on "50 years of SQC & OR in India under the theme 'Business Competitiveness and Growth Through Quantitative Methods' was organised during August 06- 08, 1998 at Chennai.

The objectives of the conference was (i) to review the development and application of SQC & OR in India since the visit of Prof. Walter Shewhart during November 1947- March 1948 (ii) to have a look at the current scenario in the development and application of SQC & OR in Indian Organisations (iii) to discuss the possibility of an interface between Industry & Academia and chart out future directions for the Division. Sixteen parallel technical sessions were arranged covering topics like Business process Improvement, Operations Research, Quality Management, Taguchi Methods among others. Significantly ISI was made a permanent member of the "Quality Council" by Govt. of India in August, 1998.

During the current period the division associated with more than 200 organisations including (i) manufacturing organisations like HMT, (Die Casting Division), ITL MICO, TAFE, WIPRO FLUID POWER, SPICER (INDIA), GABRIEL (INDIA), AUTOLIV, STUMPP, SCHUELE & SOMAPPA, IFB, RHW INDIA, HEWLETT PACKARD, BPL LIMITED, BHEL, RITES, HAL (Aircraft Division), KEC, Tumkur, KEC, (Unit V), GabBriel India Ltd., Triton Valves, Mysore, Tungabhadra Steel Products Ltd., Hospet, Aspect Development Pvt. Ltd., Tata Refractories Ltd., Steelco Gujarat Ltd., Asea Brown Boveri, Aspect Development (India) Ltd., Institute of Research in Wood Science, SRMT, Kakinada, Kinetic Engineering Ltd., Ahmednagar, Balmer-Lawrie, ICI Ltd., Coats of India, Larsen and Toubro, Tribeni Tissues, Kirlosker Electric, Motorela, ABB, BMV, Tata Tea, Mahindra &

Mahindra Ltd. (Traeter Division), Reliance Industries Ltd., Tata SSL Limited, Godrej & Boyee Mfg. Co., DCL Polyester Ltd., Technova Imaging systems Ltd., (ii) Research Institutions like Institute of chemcal Technology, Centre for cellular and Molecular Biology, National Remote Sensing Agencies and National Geophysical Research Institutes, (iii) Service organisation like Peerless Hospital.

Besides conducting the academic and professional programmes more than 125 training programmes in the area of quality management, ISO 9000 QAS, SPC and SQC, New Seven Tools, FMEA & FTA, Quality in Design & Engineering, Statistical Techniques like applied regression modellings; principal component analysis etc. were organised for individual as well as for industry groups.

Some of the areas where research were undertaken and papers published and presented were Minimisation of Loss in Steel Plant, Optimum Continuous Sampling Plans, Sensitivity of S.N. Ratio, Collinearity of Linear Models, Weighing Designs, Defect Interference, Modelling of Road Traffic Noise Data, Symmetric and completely mixed games, Complernentarity Problems.

Library, documentation and information sciences division

The Institute maintains a central research Library at Calcutta with a holding of above 2 lakhs volumes of books and bound periodicals. It has a good collection of microfiches, microfilms and photofilms. It renders regular documentation service to the Institute Scientists. It has also a well equipped Reprography and Photography Unit with facilities for an modem copying arrangement. The unit provided 4,60,849 xerox prints, 1,50,000 offsets, 500 frames of scientific photographs and 2000 prints of photographic enlargement for the users during the period.

The reading room of the Library have accommodation for about 200 readers. The services of the Library are extended to bonafide students, scholars and academic staff members of educational and scientific Institutions of the city and its neighbouring regions.

The Library maintains contacts with research Libraries of the country through inter-library loan transactions. The Library has also an excellent collection of rare and out of print books, official reports and data books of various governments and international agencies and Russian language publications.

A separate collection of books and journals is being developed for a Regional Library for Eastern Zone as "NBHM collection" funded by National Board of Higher Mathematics Dept. of Atomic Energy, Govt. of India. To provide information support and increase efficiency of library services, the Central Library at Calcutta has started the process of providing computerised library services. Projects undertaken by the library are Reclassification of books on Mathematics and Statistics, Development of Computerised Catalogue, Identification and Selective Rectification of Gaps in Periodical Collection - Development of Computer Accessible Database. The Institute also maintains two branch Libraries at Delhi and Bangalore Centre. National Board of Higher Mathematics, Department of Atomic Energy, Govt. of India has recognised Indian Statistical Institute, Delhi Centre Library as the Regional Library to serve the Northern Region since 1.4.1994.

Computer and statistical research centre (CSSC)

The centre manages the central computing facility of the Institute at Calcutta. It serves about 400 users-students, research scholars and scientific workers—with the inhouse computer system VAX 8650 and SUN SPARCSTATION 1. NSSO and CSO (I-S wing), Govt. of

India, are also using the computational facilities available in the Centre. There are external users from other scientific Institutions as well. CSSC maintains an archive of NSSO survey data for users in the eastern region of the country. E-mail, Internet and Fax facilities of the Institute are maintained by the Centre. Statistical and computational consultancy services are also provided by CSSC.

The staff members of CSSC also served as faculty in various courses of the Institute and guided projects carried out by students. They also conducted research in the areas of Data Mining, Cryptology and Temporal Data Model.

Project work

Apart from theoretical and experimental plan research, the Institute also undertook a variety of 50 externally funded projects from different Government and non-Government organisations like Dept. of Science and Technology (DST); Central Scientific and Industrial Research (CSIR), University Grants Commission (UGC), Defence Electronics Applications Laboratory (DEAL); National Information System for Science & Technology (NISSAT); Deptt. of Biotechnology (DBT), Govt. of India-, Central Silk Board, Govt. of India, Defence Research Development Organisation (DRDO); Calcutta Metropolitan Development Authority (CMDA), Ministry of Environment and Forests, Govt. of India (aided by World Bank); Directorate General of Employment and Training, Ministry of Labour, Govt. of India; Dept. of Electronics, Govt. of India; Motorola India Electronics Ltd., University of East Anglia, UK; International Rice Research Institute (IRRI), Philippines; United Nations Child Education Fund (UNICEF); Calcutta Municipal Corporation; Gramaphone Company of India (HMV); Ministry of Welfare, Govt. of India, Rabindra Bharati

University, Paschim Banga Rajya Prathamic Siksha Unnayan Sanstha, Govt. of India; Hindustan Fertilizer Corporation Ltd. (HFCL) etc.

Seminars, workshops, conferences, symposia etc.

A number of Seminars, Workshops, Conferences, Symposia, Summer Schools, Winter Schools, Training Programmes etc. were organised by the Institute during the period at Calcutta, Delhi, Bangalore etc. with the participation of distinguished scientists from India and abroad.

Publication

Founded and edited by Professor P.C. Mahalanobis in 1933, 'Sankhya', the Indian Journal of Statistics and the Official organ of the Indian Statistical Institute is now published bimonthly in two series - Sr. A on Probability and Mathematical Statistics, and Sr. B on Statistical Methodology and Applications including Sample Surveys and Quantitative Economics. Since its inception, eminent scholars all over the World have been contributing research articles for publication in Sankhya, one of the most prestigious and internationality renowned journal.

The following issues were published during the year :

— Sankhya Sr. A.- Volume 60, part 2 & 3 and Volume 6 1, Part I

— Sankhya Sr.B : Volume 60, part 1, 2 and 3.

Scientific assignments abroad

About fifty scientists of the Institute visited a number of foreign countries either on invitation or under cultural exchange programme to attend international Seminars and Conferences. Most of them presented scientific papers and delivered lectures in those Seminars and Conferences. Countries visited by ISI faculty members were USA, UK, Hungary, Japan, Italy, France, Canada,

Australia, Germany, Finland, Iran, Turkey, Thailand, Bangladesh, Indonesia, Tokyo, Sweden, South Africa, Hong Kong, Geneva, Slovenia, Singapore Kuwait, Netherlands, Brazil, Poland, Philippines, Paris, Mexico etc.

Visiting scientists

About fifty distinguished scientists from USA, UK, Italy, Canada, Japan, China, Belgium, Israel, France, Philippines etc. visited the Institute to attend various Workshops, Conferences, Seminars etc. and also to participate in the research, teaching, training and other scientific activities of the Institute. Several scientists from Indian Academic Institutions also visited the Institute in connection with the same.

Recognition to ISI scientists

In appreciation and recognition of the high standard of research and scientific excellence maintained by the researchers of the Institute, several faculty members received laurels in the forms of Awards, Fellowship from Institute/organisation of national and international importance like CSIR, NASA, IEEE, INSA, IAPRS, FNAE, etc. As usual, several faculty members served as visiting scientist, honorary professor, visiting professor, C.V. Raman Professor of INSA, Visiting Professor in the Purdue University, USA, University of Washington, USA; Institute of La Ricerca Di Base, Italy-, Indian Council of Social Sciences Research (ICSSR); Indian National Science Academy etc. Besides, many faculty members were invited by national and international Institute/bodies to act as Chairman, member, chief editor, editor for their several committees/editorial board etc.

6

Economic Development and Planning

Planning is not only an instrument of economic growth but it is accepted by all that it is an instrument of social integration. Indian society consists of many social groups both in caste, community and ethnic terms. During the national movement it was realized that political mobilization has to be done in the context of the castes and community terms. That is why Gandhi is known as a political fold. Their participation fold. Their participation in the political movement brought their economic and social needs into sharp focus. Any planning has to recognize their needs. As such, the Indian Donstitution has recognized these social groups. They are socially and economically backward. They do not have access to modern education and social services. Planning as a concept was developed during the national movement. The democratic experiment of India has to take into account the needs of SCs/STs and the OBCs. It is mandatory.

Planning is an integral part of our political culture. Strengthening democracy is possible with planning,. Planning accepts the role of State in the market economy. The role of the State is to reduce the regional disparity. It is to reduce the income disparity between various sections of our society. Liberalization process has restricted the role of the State in the area of industrialization. The private capital is today strong enough to stand on its own feet. Withdrawing the State from economic activities is a welcome step. But historical experience of the Third World countries show that the first decade of economic liberalization generated lot of economic distress. The approach paper to the Ninth Five Year Plan document has recognized this new development.

First, the regional disparity between poorer regions and richer areas has increased. Regional disparity has created already a lot of political mobilization on ethnic line.

Secondly, investment in agriculture has slowed down during this phase which sustains a majority of our people to earn their livelihood. Even after 50 years of industrialization, our agriculture is not self-sustaining. It needs State intervention for its growth. The lack of agricultural growth has reduced the employment opportunities that is reflected in the rise of unemployment and underemployment in rural India and which has pushed them to overcrowd the cities. As a result, it has increased urban poverty. Both rural and urban poverty have a close relationship.

Thirdly, urban areas are facing the crisis, in terms of providing drinking water and sanitation where the urban poor are living.

Fourthly, the decade of economic liberalization has increased the number of poor, people below the poverty line. Who are these poor people in the rural areas and urban slums? They are nobody except the people from the SCs/STs and the lower OBCs. These social classes are today the worst victims of the economic process.

The approach paper to the Ninth Plan has looked into the factors explained in the above paragraphs. It demands the reorientation of the State role and definite thrust on the poverty alleviation and employment generation without which the poor are going to distrust the democratic system. Once alienation of these communities from the system starts growing, then the system itself is going to be vulnerable.

Era of reform

The year 1991 marks a watershed in the economic history of India, as the country went through a paradigm shift-from one of the most highly regulated economies of the world which was essentially inward-looking to a market-oriented system, reducing the role of Government in making economic decisions, as the means to achieve higher growth of the economy and its rapid integration with the rest of the world.

An economic stabilisation programme and structural reforms covering trade, industry, taxation, financial sector and capital market were put through turning the worst economic crisis that confronted India since Independence into an opportunity to usher in a quiet revolution which would enable the country to attain a trajectory of higher growth and, along with it, social equity.

Developments in the Gulf region in 1990 exerted pressures on India's balance of payments and with outflow of capital, mainly NRI deposits, the foreign exchange reserves declined to about one billion dollars (barely two weeks of imports) in June 1991. The country was for the first time on the verge of defaulting on its external debt. There was no choice but to have recourse to a structural adjustment programme with the International Monetary Fund providing a standby credit for a stabilisation programme coupled with wide-ranging reforms.

The first steps were in the area of Trade Policy by devaluing the rupee by 22 per cent in dollar terms, eliminating export subsidy and reducing import licensing restrictions. A dual exchange rate system was ushered in but by March 1993, it was unified and a fully floating exchange rate regime in which the exchange rate is determined by market forces of demand and supply came into being. The foreign exchange market was widened and deepened, and in August 1994, the rupee was made fully convertible on current account, trade and non-trade. The downward adjustment of the rupee was designed to improve the country's international competitiveness and correct the imbalances in trade and current accounts.

Beginning with the 1991-92 Budget, Government also launched a phased reduction of import tariff bringing down the maximum from 300 per cent in 1990 to 50 per cent by march 1995. The changes resulted in lowering the import-weighted average tariff from 87 per cent in 1991 to 27 per cent in March 1995. The dispersion of tariffs was also significantly reduced and quantitiative restrictions were substantially eased. The trade reforms undertaken from 1991 helped to reduce the anti-export bias of Indian industry which was being exposed to both domestic and international competition.

The thrust of the Export-Import Policy (1992-97), made coterminus with the Eighth Five year Plan, is export promotion which is crucial for balance of payment and at the same time the Policy facilitates the import of production inputs required for sustaining increased industrial growth and exports.

Exports have responded impressively to the policy reforms and after the slowdown in the first two years under the impact of macrostabilisation measures, grew by an average of 18-19 per cent in the subsequent three years (1993-94 to 1995-96) in dollar terms. Exports have now diversified both commoditywise and countrywise with an increasing share going to the rest of Asia, particularly East and South East Asia with which India is trying to evolve increased trade and investment cooperation, given the rapid growth and the dynamism of these economies.

India's exports have undoubtedly gained from the expansion in world trade-as will be seen from the fact that a slowdown in global exports in 1996 has also effected India's exports to some extent in the current year-but the Government is confident that the export target of 38 billion dollars in 1996-97 would be achieved as against the 31.8 billion in 1995-96. A target of 75 billion dollars of exports by 2,000 A.D. has been set and this would mean maintaining an annual export growth of around 20 per cent in dollar terms over the next four years. This would facilitate a steady rise in the ratio of exports and imports in GDP and take India closer to one per cent as its share of world trade by the year 2001. Changes in the direction of India's trade from 1960-61 are brought out in Table IV.

In recent years, a largest percentage of imports are covered by exports—88 per cent in 1995-96. Imports have also increased with industry stagin a strong recovery from 1993-94 onwards to record double digitrates of growth. The higher import bill also reflects the demand for mass consumption items like pulses and edible oils apart from the growing dependence on imports of petroleum crude and products to keep pace with the rapid growth in energy use in the country.

The Economic Survey–1996—97 is a balanced appraisal of the past performance of the economy, attributing the gains to the policy of economic reform and liberalisaton, pursued during the last five years and presents a picture of cautious optimism for the future. While attributing the past gains to the policy of liberalisation, the Survey asserts that the policy would need to be pursued with greater vigour in future to carry the economy to higher growth path. It attributes "the loss of momentum" in the economy to "the marked slow down in the pace of reforms preceding and during the election period", but adds "this has been revived with a series of measures in recent months."

The Survey says "the initial spurt of reforms from 1991—92 t 1993—94 was very successful on all accounts, resulting in a jump in economic growth in 1994—95 to 7.2 per cent." It says GDP grew by 7.1 per cent in 1995—96 despite the slowdown in the momentum of reform and adds, econmic growth in 1996—97 is estimated by the CSO to be around 6.8 per cent (GDP at factor cost). The Eight Plan, it says is thus likely to end with an average growth of 6.5 per cent per annum, 0.9 per cent higher than the target rate of 5.6 per cent and 0.5 per cent point higher than the actual achievement of the Seventh Plan. More important for the future is the fact that the average growth during the latest three years is 7 per cent, probably placing India among the top ten performers in the world during the period."

However, when it comes to a review of sectoral performance that he Survey is compelled to be more realistic. It says "the economy in 1996–97 so far presents a mixed picture." Although, it says "overall economic growth remains high at 6.8 per cent, and agriculture has rebounded, the growth of manufacturing value added has slowed and the performance of key infrastructure sectors, especially power and crude oil, is weak. The annual rate of inflation (point to point) has risen t actual long—term levels and export growth has decelerated markedly in recent months."

On agriculture, the Survey says "production in 1996—97 is expected to show good recovery from the slower growth in 1995—96. The growth is projected at 3 per cent after a fall of 0.4 per cent in 1995–96. The sharp decline in foodgrains production by 3.4 per cent, which was responsible for the slow growth in 1995–96, is expected to be reversed by; an increase of 3.3 per cent in 1996—97. Foodgrains production is expected to recover to 191.2 million tonnes, only marginally lower than the level of production in 1994—95. The recovery is primarily due to coarse cereals, as well as anticipated rise in wheat production, which suffered a sharp setback in 1995—96." Commercial crop production has done extremely well in 1996—97 with oilseeds and cotton expected to reach record levels of 24.1 and 14.1 million tonnes respectively.

The momentum of growth witnessed in 1995—96 with a GDP growth of over 7 per cent, has been maintained in 1996—97, thus providing increasing evidence that the growth potential has improved as a result of the reforms initiated in 1991. With the growing participation of virtually the entire spectrum of political opinion inthe reform process, there is a good prospect that a higher growth rate would become a permanent feature of the economy.

The initial spurt of reforms from 1991—92 to 1993—94 was very successful by all accounts, resulting in a jump in economic growth to 7.2 per cent in 1994—95 (in terms of GDP at factor cost). Since 1994—95, however, there was a marked slow down in the pace of reforms. Nevertheless, GDP grew by 7.1 per cent in 1995—96. The slackening of reforms preceding and during the election period may have been responsible for some loss of momentum, but this has been revived with a series of measures in recent months.

Economic growth in 1996—97 is estimated by CSO to be around 6.8 per cent (GDP at factor cost). Thus, the Eighth Plan is likely to end with an average growth of 6.5 per cent per annum, 0.9 per cent point higher than the target rate of 5.6 per cent, and 0.5 per cent point higher than the actual achievement of the Seventh Plan. More important for the future is the fact that the average growth during the latest three years is 7 per cent, probably placing India among the top ten performers in the world during this period.

As the final year of the Eighth Plan draws to a close, a comparison of some salient dimensions of some salilent dimensions of economic performance between the Eighth Plan period and its predecessor reveals the following:

— Overall economic growth has been faster;

— The manufacturing sector has grown almost 2 per cent points faster per year in the Eighth Plan period;

— Agriculture and allied sectors have grown at about 3.5 per cent per annum in both periods;

— Both exports and imports have grown significantly faster in the Eighth Plan period;

— The balance of payments has strengthened considerably, with trade and current account deficits declining as ratios of GDP, while exports and imports have grown rapidly both in value terms as well as in proportion to GDP.

— The Central Government's fiscal deficit as a proportion of GDP has declined significantly;

— The average rate of gross domestic savings has risen substantially from 20.6 per cent of GDP in the Seventh Plan period to 23.9 per cent in the first four years of the Eighth Plan;

— With the exception of telecommunications, the rate of growth of net output (value added) of infrastructure sectors has slowed;

— The average rate of inflation has risen somewhat, though remaining below double digits.

Total gross domestic saving reached a new peak of 25.6 per cent of GDP in 1995—96, exceeding its previous peak of 24.9 per cent of GDP in 1994–95. This seems to vindicate the reform strategy of encouraging savings by expanding saving and investment opportunities, rather than giving special incentives.

Gross domestic investment (adjusted), as a proportion of GDP at current prices, rose even faster than gross domestic saving in 1995—96 to a high of 27.4 per cent from 26 per cent in the previous year. Gross domestic investment in real terms, as a proportion of GDP at constant prices, reached a new peak of 27.1 per cent, exceeding the previous peak of 25.9 per cent in 1990—91. Gross fixed capital formation which is even more important for productivity and growth, reached a new peak of 24.1 per cent of GDP in 1995—96. Private sector investment appears to have responded vigorously to the policy of promoting competition, removing policy distortions and hurdles, and improving access to factors of production (e.g. technology, capital).

Estimates of savings and investment in 1996—97 are not yet available. Indicators are mixed. On the one hand, domestic capital goods production is buoyent and disbursement of financial institutions are significantly higher, on the other hand, capital goods imports have declined, non—oil imports are lower in the first nine months of the year, corporate demand for credit appears slack, and sanctions of financial institutions are substantially lower.

The economy in 1996—97 so far presents a mixed picture in other dimensions as well. Although overall economic growth remains high at 6.8 per cent, and agriculture has rebounded, the growth of manufacturing value added has slowed and the performance of key infrastructure sectors, especially power and crude oil, is weak. The annual rate of inflation (point to point) has risen back to average long—term levels and export growth has decelerated markedly in recent months. Despite the slowdown in exports, a combination of sluggish imports and reasonably buoyant inflows of invisibles and capital flows have led to a build—up of foreign exchange reserves by over $ 2.5 billion.

In the previous chapter, we described the situation as it prevailed in 1960-61. We shall now proceed to take a brief review of the progress made during the past decade. The last year for which some data are available is 1968-69. Therefore, in the following review, we shall cover the period from 1960-61 to 1968-69.

National Income again offers a useful summary measure to judge the performance of the economy in a given period. The particular measure of national income we shall use is specifically termed Net National Product at Factor Cost. We shall briefly refer to it as NNP. We have earlier mentioned that the NNP was Rs. 13,308 crores in 1960-61. It increased to Rs. 28,800 crores in 1968-69 was 216.4. The NNP increased annually by about 6 percentage points during 1961-62 and 1962-63; by almost 17 percentage points in 1963-64; by 26 percentage points in the next two years; by 23 percentage points in 1966-67; by 32 percentage points in 1967-68; and finally, by 6 percentage points in 1968-69. Over the eight years from 1960-61 to 1968-69, the NNP more than doubled.

This is a spectacular performance if it were all real. Unfortunately it is not all real. During the eight years from 1960-61 to 1968-69, the prices of commodities have almost doubled. This means that a rupee in 1968-69 does not mean the same thing as it did in 1960-61. Hence, to judge the real increase in NNP, we should ask what would the NNP be if the prices had remained unchanged. In other words, we should value the NNP in subsequent years at prices as they prevailed in 1960-61. We shall refer to this as Net National Product at Constant (1960-61) Prices. From such a series, it becomes clear that the NNP increased by only 26.5 per cent in eight years and not by 116.4 per cnet as appeared earlier. Thus the real increase in the NNP is only 26.5 per cent in eight years; the balance of apparent increase is a reflection of the increase in prices.

The growth in the NNP has not been steady. This is because agricultural production, which constitutes almost half of the total, is still liable to wide fluctuations from year to year. The real increase in the NNP by 6 percentage points in 1963-64 and again by 8 percentage points in 1964-65 was because of the good agricultural season in those two years. This was followed by two very bad years and the NNP actually declined in 1965-66 and remained at the same low level in 1966-67. Fortunately, the year 1967-68 turned out to be a very good year and the NNP jumped by 10 percentage points. The year 1968-69 was also a good year and the NNP is estimated to have advanced by another 2 percentage points.

Thus the anunal fluctuations in agricultural production explain the unsteady growth of the NNP. But in a period as long as 8 to 10 years, one must take good years along with bad years and reckon the fact that the real increase in NNP in eight years was only 26.5 per cent which is a compound growth rate of less than 3 per cent per annum.

The growth in the NNP must be placed alongside the growth in population. The population of the Indian Union in 1961 was 434 million. We shall know what it is when the census is taken this year. However, in the meanwhile, the population is estimated to have been growing at the annual rate of 2.5 per cent. Clearly, therefore, a growth of NNP at an annual rate of no more than 3 per cent is barely sufficient to keep pace with the growth in population; it leaves little margin to make a net improvement in the economic condition of the people. This becomes clear if we divide the NNP by the estimated population each year to get the NNP per capita. If this is done, it becomes clear that the per capita NNP increased from Rs. 306.7 in 1960-61 to just Rs. 321.3 in 1967-68 and Rs. 319.4 in 1968-69. This is an increase at best of only 4.5 per cent in eight years which is about half a per cent per annum. This summarises the performance of the economy during the past decade.

As mentioned earlier, per capita private consumer expenditure gives a more direct measure of the well-being or standard of living of a people. We have seen that the per capita private consumer expenditure was Rs. 276.3 in 1960-61. In are given the relevant data for the subsequent years. In order to assess the real changes in the per capita consumer expenditure in subsequent years at constant (1960-61) prices for the years from 1960-61 to 1968-69.

It will be seen that the per capita consumer expenditure increased from Rs. 276.3 in 1960-61 to Rs. 285.5 (at 1960-61 prices) in 1968-69. The per capita consumer expenditure shows a sudden increase (Rs. 296.0) in 1964-65 and then a sudden fall (Rs. 269.8 and Rs. 271.8) in the following two years. This is a reflection of the bumper agricultural production in 1964-65 and poor production in the following two years. The average per capita consumption during the three years 1964-65, 1965-66 and 1966-67 was Rs. 279.2 per annum. It seems more likely that the real consumption was maintained more or less at this level by carrying some of the large stocks of 1964-65 into the next two years rather than allowing it to fluctuate along with fluctuations in agricultural production. For the same reason, we should smoothen out the fluctuations in the first three years as also in the last two years. When this is done, the estimates of per capita consumer expenditure in the nine years appear as shown in. They seem more reasonable and plausible.

The upshot of the whole exercise is that the per capita consumer expenditure rose from Rs. 276.3 in 1960-61 to Rs. 289.6 in 1968-69, that is by 4.8 per cent in eight years or by about half a per cent per annum. It is obvious that it could not have risen by any more because, we have seen as the per capita income rose at best by 4.5 per cent in the eight years. Incidentally, we may note that the per capita consumer expenditure seems to have increased a little more than has the per capita national income. The reasons seem to be firstly that the large increase in national income registered in the last two years has been mainly on account of the large increase in the production of foodgrains in these years and secondly that the net domestic capital formation as a proportion of the net domestic expenditure has gone down sharply in these two years.

This brings us to the next point namely how are these small gains of development distributed between different sections of the population–between the rural and urban populations and between the richer and poorer sections of these populations? More specifically, we ask: The average consumer expenditure in the country rose by 4.8 per cent in real terms (that is at constant prices) in the eight years from 1960-61 and 1968-69. Did this happen equally in the case of the rural and urban populations and equally in the case of the richer and poorer sections of these populations? These questions are crucial while assessing whether anything is happening to the poor of this country; whether their lot has improved materially as a result of the economic development of the past decade. If the per capita consumption in the country has risen by no more than 4.8 per cent in eight years, it is obvious that little noticeable could have happened in the nature of alleviation of poverty unless the poorer sections have profited proportionately more than the average and much more so than the rich. Did this happen during the past decade? We shall examine the facts.

Rural-urban differential

As mentioned earlier, the National Sample Survey (NSS) offers estimates of private consumer expenditure in rural and urban areas separately. In we give the NSS estimates of per capita consumer expenditure for the rural and urban populations for the years 1960-61 and 1967-68. In order to make the estimates for 1967-68 comparable with those for 1960-61, the estimates for 1967-68 must be expressed at prices prevailing in 1960-61. This is done in the second line of the Table.

As earlier mentioned, the NSS estimate of per capita private consumer expenditure for 1960-61 (Rs. 278.8) is in close agreement with the corresponding official estimate (Rs. 276.3); the NSS estimate is higher than the official estimate by less than one per cent (0.9 per cent). However, the NSS estimate of per capita private consumer expenditure for 1967-68 at 1960-61 prices (Rs. 256.2) is much below the corresponding official estimate (Rs. 287.0). Indeed the NSS estimate is short of the official estimate by as much as 10.7 per cent.

It seems that the NSS estimate of per capita private consumer expenditure for 1967-68 is an underestimate. This becomes clear if we compare it with the NSS estimate for 1960-61. It will be seen that, compared at constant 1960-61 prices, the NSS estimate for 1967-68 (Rs. 256.2) is below the NSS estimate for 1960-61 (Rs. 278.8) by as much as 8.1 per cent. Hence, if we rely on the NSS estimates, it would appear that the per capita consumption declined by as much as 8.1 per cent during the seven years from 1960-61 to 1967-68. This appears unlikely. Hence, we must conclude that the NSS estimate of per capita consumer expenditure in 1967-68 is in fact an underestimate.

We shall later examine the reasons for and the nature of this underestimation. For the present, we propose to revise the NSS estimates of rural and urban per capita consumer expenditure, both in 1960-61 and 1967-68, in order to bring them in accord with the official estimates of per capita national consumption in those years. * It will be noticed that the revision is only slight for 1960-61 but is very considerable for 1967-68.

From the estimates of per capita rural and urban consumer expenditure thus revised, it will be seen that the per capita national consumer expenditure increased from Rs.276.3 in 1960-61 to Rs. 287.0 in 1967-68 that is by 3.9 per cent. In the same period, the per capita rural consumer expenditure increased from Rs. 258.8 to Rs. 268.6 that is by 3.8 per cent, while the per capita urban consumer expenditure increased from Rs. 356.4 to Rs. 364.9 that is by 2.4 per cent. Thus it seems that the average consumption in the rural area has improved a little more, though only slightly, than the average consumptions in urban area. Consequently, the rural-urban difference has been reduced a little. For instance, in 1960-61, the per capita urban consumption (Rs. 356.4) was 37.7 per cent higher than the per capita rural consumptions (Rs. 258.8). In 1967-68, the per capita urban consumption (Rs. 364.9) was only 35.9 per cent higher than the per capita rural consumption. We shall later examine the process through which the rural-urban difference has been thus reduced, even if only slightly.

Overall economic growth in terms of Gross Domestic Product (GDP) at constant factor cost improved from 0.8% in 1991-92 to 6.3% in 1994-95 and 7% in 1995-96 aided by a growth rate of 2.4% by agriculture and allied sectors, 11.7% by industry and construction sector and 7% by services. Overall economic growth during the first four year of the 8th Plan (1992-97) averaged 5.9% per annum compared with the planned target of 5.6%.

The domestic savings rate measured in terms of gross domestic savings as a proportion of GDP at current market prices increased from an average rate of 21.3% in 1992-93 and 1993-94 to 24.4% in 1994-95. The rate of domestic investment measured in terms of gross domestic capital formation as a proportion of GDP at current market prices increased from 21.6% in 1993-94 to 25.2% in 1994-95.

Industrial production which was virtually stagnant in 1991-92 increased by 9.4% and 12.1% in 1995-96 supported by a growth rate of 6.9% in mining, 13.6% in manufacturing and 8.1% in electricity generation. As per the latest information available, industrial growth deceleration to 8.5% in April-June 1996 due to deceleration of growth rates in all the sub-sectors (3.6% in mining, 10.4% manufacturing and 2.2% in electricity generation). As per growth rates by use-based classification, capital goods sector recorded a growth rate of 14.2%, intermediate goods 11.9%, consumer durables 11.1% and consumer non-durables 8.6% in April-June 1996. However, the growth rate of basic goods sub-sector having a weight of 39.4% in the overall industrial production was only 4% in April-June 1996.

Seven infrastructural sectors, namely, electricity, coal, steel, cement, crude oil and petroleum product & fertilizer with a combined weight of 31% in the Index of Industrial Production (IIP) recorded a growth rate of 7.8% in 1995-96. But their growth rate decelerated to 3.2% in April-August 1996 due to poor performance of electricity generation (growth rate of only 2.4%) and crude oil production (decline of production by 10.4%).

The outlook of agricultural production in 1996-97 is excellent with foodgrains output likely to reach 197 million tonnes compared with 185 million tonnes in 1995-96. This is primarily due to this year's rainfall distribution being the best in the past five years. The late withdrawal of monsoon has further ensured bright prospects for rabi production this year.

The estimate of foodgrains production in 1995-96 has been scaled down to 185 million tonnes representing a sharp decline of nearly 6 million tonnes over the prec * eeding year. The shortfall was substantial (about 3 million tonnes) in wheat output, besides short-fall of production of rice and coarse cereals. Consequently wheat procurement dropped steeply to 8.2 million tonnes compared to 12.3 million tonnes in the preceding year. Public stock (Central Pool) of foodgrains was about 22.1 million tonnes as on September 1, 1996.

Economic census and surveys

The Central Statistical Organisation (CSO) conducted the first economic census in 1977 to bridge the data gaps in the unorganised sectors of non-agricultural economy. The economic census was aimed at providing basic information on distribution of non-agricultural enterprises and to provide a frame for follow-up surveys for collection of detailed information about the structure of enterprises, investments, input, output, emploument, etc. The first economic census was followed by two sample surveys-one in 1978-79 relating to unorganised manufacturing and the second in 979-80 devoted to trade, transport, hotels and restaurants, storage and warehousing and services.

The second Economic Census was conducted in 1980 during the houselisting operations of 1981 Population Census with increased scope and coverage. It covered all enterprises (establishments and own-account enterprises) in the non-agricultural sector excluding crop production and plantation. Based on the information thrown up by this Census, three follow-up surveys were carried out, one in 1983-84 on hotels and restaurants, transport, storage and warehousing and services; second in 1984-85 on unorganised manufacturing and third in 1985-86 on wholesale and retail trade. The frame of 1980 Census was updated during 1987-88 in 64 towns. On the basis of Economic Census 1980 and updated frame, four sample surveys were conducted.

The third Economic Census 1990 was conducted along with the houselisting operations of 1991 Population Census in all states/union territories except Jammu and Kashmir. The data processing of Economic Census 1990 was undertaken in a decentralised manner by state/ union territories. Some of the states/union territories utilised the services of Regional Computer Centres at Calcutta and Chandigarh. The all India results of Economic Census 1990 brought out shortly by the CSO for which processing and tabulation has been done by the Computer Centre, Department of SAtatistics. On the basis of the frame thrown up by Economic Census 1990, a follow-up survey covering sectors of mining and quarrying and storage and warehousing was conducted during 1992-93 and another survey on hotels and restaurants and transport was conducted during January to September, 1994.

According to 1980 Economic Census, there were 18.4 million enterprises in the country (excluding Assam) employing 53.6 million persons. Among these, these were 16.9 million enterprises (58.4 per cent in rural areas) engaged in non-agricultural activitties employing 50.7

million persons (43.3 per cent in rural areas). As per of the results of Economic Census 1990, there were 25 million enterprises out of which 22.7 million were in the non-agricultural sector. The total number of persons usually working were of the order of 72.1 million out of which 40.2 million were hired workers. A total of 17.7 million enterprises operated without any hired labour on a regular basis and were mainly run by the households themselves.

Ministry of Finance is responsible for administration of finances of the Government. It is concerned with all economic and financial matters affecting the country as a whole including mobilisation of resources for development and other purposes. It regulates expenditure of Government including transfer of resources to the states. This Ministry comprises three departments, namely, (i) Economic Affairs, (ii) Expenditure and (iii) Revenue.

The Department of Economic Affairs consists of seven main divisions namely, (i) Economic, (ii) Banking, (iii) Insurance, (iv) Budget, (v) Investment, (vi) External Finance and (vii) Currency and Coinage. This Department inter alia monitors current economic trends and advises Government on all matters of internal and external economic management including working of commercial banks, term-lending institutions, investments regulations, external assistance, etc. Preparation of the Budget of the Union of India as well as the state governments and union territory administrations with legislature when under President's rule and their presentation to Parliament is also the responsibility of this Department.

The Department of Expenditure comprises eight main divisions, namely, (i) Plan finance Division, (ii) Establishment Division, (iii) Cost Accounts Branch, (iv)

Controller General of Accounts, (v) Finance Commission Division, (vi) Implementation Cell, (vii) Integrated Finance Division and (viii) Staff Inspection Unit.

Department of Revenue exercises control in respect of revenue matters relating to direct and indirect Union taxes through two statutory boards namely, Central Board of Direct Taxes and the Central Board of Excise and Customs. This Department-is also entrusted with the administration and enforcement of controls and regulatory measures provided in the enactments concerning Central sales tax, stamp duties, gold control, foreign exchange and other relevant fiscal statutes. Control over production and disposal of opium and its products is also vested with this Department.

The Finance Minister Mr. P. Chidambaram presented an innovative, well—balanced and virtually a tax—free budget for 1997—98, which should boost savings and investment and help the economy to bounce back with vigour. Many of Mr. Chidambaram's proposals were on expected lines, but his comprehensive package would be received with aplomb all round because of his demonstrated commitment to contain fiscal deficit and advance the reform process.

Undoubtedly, the Finance Minister must have been greatly concerned over the industrial slowdown and the prolonged sluggishness of the capital market, which will now get a shot—in—the—arm by the range of his tax and non—tax measures.

The Corporate sector must be more than satisfied with the Finance Minister's response to their oftrepeated suggestions while tax—payers in general would get substantial relief from across—the—board lowering of rates. Mr. Chidambaram hopes to restore buoyancy to direct tax revenues so as to raise the tax—GDP ratio and the share of direct taxes in the total tax revenues of

Government. He has sought to widen the base of taxation by making it obligatory on residents of large metropolitan areas owning vehicle, telephone or immovable property to file tax returns. A new simplified scheme is being introduced for retail traders to evoke better compliance replacing the presumptive tax scheme which did not yield the desired results.

To harness black money for productive purposes, especially infrastructure, and for financing the Basic Minimum Services Programme he has announced a voluntary disclosure of income and wealth scheme with certain immunity for those coming forward to disclose their cash holdings or assets. The scheme will be in force till the end of 1997.

As expected, Mr. Chidambaram not only abolished the remaining 7.5 per cent surcharge but also reduced the corporate tax rate to 35 per cent while foreign companies would bear 48 per cent. The rate reduction for foreign companies coupled with the decision to raise the aggregate limit of investment in a company by institutional investors from 24 to 30 per cent should attract larger flows of both direct and portfolio investments. For non—resident Indians, the capital gains tax arising on transfer of securities has been reduced to 10 per cent bringing them on par with foreign institutional investors.

Apart from fulfilling his promise to limit fiscal deficit to 5 per cent of GDP in the current year, Mr. Chidambaram has kept the deficit in 1997—98 at 4.5 per cent with a hope of further lowering it to under 4 per cent in the next budget. This would have a salutary impact on the international investor community.

Adhering to his undertaking last year, Mr. Chidambaram has announced the phasing out of the system of ad hoc treasury bills, which have been used to monestise the budget deficits, from April 1st this year. Instead, a scheme of ways and means advances by the Reserve Bank of India to the Central Government is being introduced to take care of mismatches in government's receipts and payments. Mr. Chidambaram has assured that this would not become a permanent source of financing budgetary deficits. Details of the scheme are being announced by the Reserve Bank. The RBI will, however, continue to support government's borrowing programme and the budget for 1997–98 assumes a limit of Rs. 16000 crore for such support. Mr. Chidambaram described the new arrangement as a bold and radical change, intended to strengthen fiscal discipline and also provide greater autonomy to the Reserve Bank in the conduct of monetary policy. The conventional budget deficit has now lost its relevance and the Gross Fiscal Deficit will become the key indicator of total deficit. The Finance Minister has announced that he would introduce a new instrument of capital indexed bonds to provide investors an effective hedge against inflation.

In the spirit of cooperative fedetalism embodied in the Common Minimum Programme of the United Front Government, the Finance Minister has accepted the Tenth Finance Commission's recommendation for a single, divisible pool of taxes to be shared between the Centre and the States. He said Government would adopt the proportion of 29 per cent recommended by the Commission. However, this matter would have to be the subject matter of a constitutional amendment and many States are pleading for a much higher percentage of devolution than the 29 per cent the Fnance Commission has recommended.

Along with fiscal adjustment, Mr. Chidambaram has given a definite push to the reform process, which had slowed down before process, which had slowed down before and after last year's elections to the Lok Sabha. On the much awaited stand of Government on private sector entering the insurance business, Mr. Chidambaram has come up with a limited opening in the areas of pension business and health insurance. The Life Insurance and General Insurance Corporations will continue to enjoy their monopoly over life and non—life and non—health insurance business.

But companies with majority Indian ownership and control will be permitted to enter health insurance, GIC and LIC can also have joint ventures in pension and health insurance business.

Though Mr. Chidambaram did not refer to any restructuring of public sector enterprises, he said, Government would delegate more managerial and commercial autonomy to all public undertakings. Nine well performing enterprises would be helped to become global giants. Though disinvestment in public undertakings did not take off in 1996—97, the Finance Minister has endorsed the Disinvestment Commission's scheme of disinvestment on the basis of their periodical reports. The budget for the coming year expects to realise Rs. 4800 crore from disinvestment.

In his budget speech, the Finance Minister also announced a new oil exploration licensing policy, under which companies like Oil and Natural Gas Corporation and oil India Limited, will be paid international price of oil for new discoveries. Royalty payments will be fixed on an ad—valorem basis.

The companies will have freedom for marketing crude oil and gas in the domestic market. tax holidays, duty concessions and abolition of cess for the new exploration blocks are provided for in the new policy. Mr. Chidambaram hoped that Indian and foreign companies would respond positively to the new policy which will include a separate tax code to facilitate new investments. Oil exploration and industrial parks will qualify for five year tax holiday in addition to telecommunications.

It is rarely that a Finance Minister gets encomiums from various sectoins of the society for his budget proposals. But Mr. P. Chidambaram has managed to achieve such kudos with his budget proposals for 1997–98. The capital market, the corporate sector as well as the ordinary salaried class have al welcomed his proposals, as Mr. Chidambaram has tried to give something to all of them in the hope that they will all be enthused to help him raise more resources to be ploughed back into the economy.

Of course, the former Finance Minister, Dr. Manmohan Singh, who was the architect of initiating the current economic reforms policy in 1991, has said that the euphoria over the budget proposals may not last if the present government was unable to muster a consensus for resolving certain contentious macro—economic issues. But even he is forced to admit that the most significant element of Mr. Chidambaram's budget is that India has not given up on reforms. Dr. Singh has also appreciated the direction of reform in indirect taxes and restructuring of customs duty proposed in the budget.

Mr. Chidambaram's task was not an easy one. He happens to be the Finance Minister in a coalition government formed by 13 parties and supported by a major party from outside. Even in the best of times, no Finance Minister can be have his way entirely while farming the budget proposals, as he has to take the entire Cabinet along. So Mr. Chidambaram's situation can be better appreciated.

Moreover he was presenting the budget at a time when the picture on the industrial fronts as well as on exports was not rosy. The capital market has been down for months (the sensitive index of the Mumbai stock exchange touched a three—year low last december). Industry in general had its misgiving on many crucial issues. The morale was rather low all round.

In a situation like this, Mr. Chidambaram had to do something which will psychologically lift the morale of various groups. This boosting up of the psychological morale is what he has done successfully through some bold proposals in the 1997–98 budget.

Now to analyse some of the major proposals contained in the budget. Mr. Chidambaram outlines his approach and says that "a good tax policy should aim at moderate rates, a widex tax base, simpler procedural rules and securing greater compliance. Households and the corporate sector are our best savers; we must reward them."

With this objective in mind, he has rationalised the personal income–tax structure, keeping the rate at the lowest slab at 10 per cent and the highest at 30 per cent (as against 15 per cent and 40 per cent respectively so far). He has also increased the standard deduction to Rs. 20,000 and has proposed that senior citizens having income upto Rs. 1,00,000 would not have to pay any tax. Thus with one stroke he has earned the gratitude of 12 million people who are assessed to income tax now.

To broaden the net wider, he has proposed that in future those who satisfy any of the two following economic criteria—ownership of a four–wheeler vehicle, a telephone, a house or have undertaken foreign travel in the previous year—should voluntarily file their tax returns. No one can seriously object to this proposals; but in attempting to widen the tax base, one hopes the government will ensure that unnecessary harassment is avoided.

Of course, the Finance Minister has introduced a voluntary disclosure scheme to harness black money. The measure has naturally created some controversy and entical questions have been raised. It remains to be seen how far the present scheme—which is different from similar schemes introduced earlier—is successful.

After trying to win the confidence of the individual tax payer, Mr. Chidambaram turns his attention next to the corporate sector. By abolishing the 7.5 per cent surcharge on corporate tax and reducing the rate of taxation for domestic companies to 35 per cent and for foreign companies to 48 per cent, he has conceded one of the long–term demands of industry.

His proposal in the 1996–97 budget for a Minimum Alternate tax (MAT) had some sections of industry u in arms. By now exempting export profits from MAT and bringing about modifications in the application of MAT, he has assuaged the feelings created by his last year's proposal.

Another major concession Mr. Chidambaram has given is the abolition of tax on corporate dividends in the hands of the shareholders. This single proposal, along with abolition o fthe surcharge on corporate tax and MAT modifications, has been such a morale booster for the capital market that the Mumbai stock sensitive index gained over 400 points in two trading days after the presentation of the budget.

Other proposals specifically aimed at improving the sentiment of the stock markets include acceptance in principle of buy–back of share by companies subject to certain conditions and the one–time permission to stockbrokers to corporatise their businesses without attracting tax on capital gains. Companies raising funds from the capital market will be required to give an annual statement disclosing the end—use of such funds.

This is intended to restore the faith of small investors in stocks. With regard to indirect taxes also, Mr. Chidambaram has taken some bold measures which have all been welcomed by industry in general. He has outlined that the goal was to achieve the average level of tariffs prevalent in ASEAN countries by the turn of the century. This will give time to Indian industry adjust to these changes. With that objective in mind, he has reduced the peak rate of customs duty from 50 per cent to 40 per cent.

He has reduced the duty on capital goods from 25 to 20 per cent and added that over the next two to three years, these rates would need to be further adjusted to conform to levels prevalent in other developing Asian countries.

Duties have been reduced on raw materials used by steel, chemical and textile industries. Stating that "if there is one science that will dominate the 21st century, it is the information technology and if there is one industry in which India can emerge as a world leader, it is the information technology," Mr. Chidambaram has given a number of concessions to encourage this industry.

Tourism is a major foreign exchange earner and there are specific proposals to boost investment in this sector. Coupled with the abolition of surcharge on corporate tax, one should see some surge in investment in this industry.

Like in customs duty, the Fnance Minister has given across the board concessions in central excise also. Last July, he said, he had promised that within three years "we shall have a four—rate tax structure." With this objective in view, he has introduced three rates—8 per cent, 13 per cent and 18 per cent. Jute industry has been given a special treatment, as he has exempted all jute and jute products from excise duty, Excise duty has been cut in respect of several items of mass consumption.

The 1997—98 Union Budget has broken new grounds in terms of carrying forward the liberalisation process and tax reforms by attempting to impart growth impulses to the economy. The Budget initiatives are important for more reasons than one presumably because the macro economic parameters of the economy were onthe downswing throughout most of the last year of the Eighth Plan (1997—98) with inflation rearing its head, trends in industrial production and foreign trade remaining none too ecouraging and capital markets coasting on thin trading for even blue chip companies. The 1997—98 Budget, as such, was expected to address these serious maladies so as to ensure that the economic activity gathered momentum and also to herals hope for realising the seven per cent growth target set for the Ninth Plan for which 1997–98 Budget is the inaugural year.

The Finance Minister Mr. P. Chidambaram did not dash hopes on all these things as the Budget he presented was a deft exercise in attempting to satisfy every constituency—be it salaried class, trade and industry, investors, both domestic and foreign and instiitutionals. In a master stroke, the Finance Minister attempted to rope in only one segment under the tax net and that is the services sector which is now contributing 40 per cent to the GDP. The logic is that "services" are products as much as "manufactured goods" and it was historic underestimation of this segment that had led to the neglect of any attempt to bring this into the tax net. But the credit for bringing services under the tax net must redound to the glory of the reform architect Dr. Manmohan Singh who initiated a modest but momentous beginning by introducing services tax on telephones and stock brokerage. Later, it was extended t advertising, courier and radio paging. From nowhere, the services tax fetched Rs. 970 crore for the exchequer in the fiscal year 1996—97.

It is but natural that the 1997—98 Union Budget should extend the services tax to some more aeas. The Finance Minister did not hesitate to do so and in his second budget after assuming office in July 1996, Mr. P. Chidambaram has confined his tax mobilisation effort to mop up Rs. 1205 crore only by bringing a few more services under the tax net and revising postal rates. The Budget for 1997—98 extends the service tax to cover a host of well–known services embracing transportation of goods by road, consulting engineers, custom house, steamer and clearing and forwarding agents, air travel agents, tour operators and car rental agencies, out—door caterers, pandal contractors and mandap keepers and man—power recruitment agencies. While the proposals on service tax are estimated to yield a revenue of Rs. 1200 crore in a full year, in the next fiscal year, a credit of Rs. 900 crore alone is being taken into account. The remaineder Rs. 305 crore for next year is being realised by revision of tariffs for some postal services, the proceeds of which would be for the development of postal services and in partially bridging the deficit on the numerous services being provided by the Postal Department.

A particularly noteworthy feature of the 1997—98 Budget is that it has given away massive customs tax relief amounting to Rs. 2625 crore and the reason for that as provided by the Finance Minister was that "our goal must be to achieve rapid and broad–based growth." While Mr. P. Chidambaram reduced the peak rate of customs duty from 50 to 40 per cent in a bid to align the country's tariff structure with international standards, he also reduced customs duty on capital goods from 20 to 15 per cent. Some of the intermediate inputs which witnessed cuts include steel industry inputs, cold rolled coils of iron andsteel, duty on ships brought for breaking, organic and inorganic chemicals, dyes, pigments, paints and varnishes, glues, enzymes and modified starches.

In tune with the tenet of emerging cooperative federalism, which is the hall—mark of the 13—party coalition government at the Centre, the Budget has accepted the alternative devolution formula seeking to bring in all taxes collected bythe Centre into a single divisible pool and apportion 29 per cent to the States as recommended by the Tenth Finance Commission.

The Budget of 1997—98 is a veritable bag of sops for Indian corporates and tax—payers as duty was cut across—the—board. In personal income tax, the existing rates of 15, 30 and 40 per cent is proposed to be replaced by 10, 20 and 30 per cent. The rate would be 10 per cent in the slab of Rs. 40,000 to Rs. 60,000, 20 per cent in the slab of Rs. 60,000 to Rs. 15,000 and 30 per cent for all income above Rs. 150,000. The limit on standard deductions has been raised to Rs. 20,000 which would apply uniformly to all salaried tax payers. In widening the tax net, the Budget proposed an amendment of Section 139 of the I.T. Act by which residents of large metropolises who satisfy economic criteria such as ownership of a four–wheel vehicle, telephone, flats and undertaking foreign travel in the previous year should voluntarily file their tax returns. Failure to do so would entail a simple notice from the I.T. Department. Yet another related scheme announced in the Budget pertains to the Voluntary Disclosure Scheme (VDS). Following the mandate of the National Development Council (NDC), the Minister announced the VDS to tap black money for productive purposes by which any disclosed income would be taxed at the revised highest rate of 30 per cent, the states would receive 77.5 of the proceeds on this score while the balance would be spent on bolstering the Basic Minimum Services. The scheme would start on a date to be notified by the Finance Minister and end on December 31, 1997. Some category of people would not be liable to secure immunity under this scheme and they include those held for offences under the Drugs and Psychotropic Substances, Arms Act, ordinarily punishable under the IPC and the Anti—Corruption Act.

A reappraisal of the country's Science and Technology (S&T) policy is called for in the wake of economic liberalization and the emerging globalization research and development (R&D) The basic object of the reappraisal would be to provide better assistance to the country's industrial growth and exports, industrial growth and exports, besides enhancing the quality of life of the people.

Several eminent scientists and technocrats have highlighted the inadequacies of the current approach to S & T. The government's S & T policy has been termed "short sighted" at the recent 84th session of the Indian Science Congress. In the words of a well-known scientist, if the government went on "underplaying S & T at it has been doing since the economic reforms started", there would be hardly any science left in this country in another 5-10 years.

Main issues

Though S & T is to be given high priority in the Ninth Plan, it should address several fundamental problems hindering its effective application. A brief overview of the main issues that need to be addressed would reveal several soft options but few hard choices for the planners.

The country' R&D expenditure declined from a little over one per cent to 0.86 per cent of the gross national product (GNP) during 1990-95 and the trend has not been reversed. Though this is relatively high among developing countries, it is very small compared with 2.5 per cent of GNP spent by developed countries in general. India's R&D expenditure is around $ 1 billion. The

United States spends 200 times more than India on R&D, while Japan and South Korea allot 140 times more. Though we have the third largest manpower with some science and technology qualification, we do not have any advantage in terms of specialized skills and training.

No doubt the Plan allocation for S&T has considerably increased from Rs. 15 crore in the I Plan to Rs. 9,180 crore in the VIII Plan. However, a major share has gone to Defence, Space and Atomic Energy. For example, the 1995-96 budget estimates of the Departments of Atomic Energy and Space were Rs. 1,001 crore and Rs. 911 crore, respectively.

More than money, young people today shy away from science. In 1950-51, there were 1,27,000 students enrolled in the science stream and in 1993, we have 10 million of them. But, the percentage of students opting for science at the undergraduate level was 32 in 1950-51, which declined to 19 in 1993. Again, the top 32 per cent opted for science in 1950, but today only the middle and the lower 19 go for it. Management, accountancy and financial disciplines attract more. Computer software is the lone exception in terms of popularity but the numbers for employment will soon become limited, especially at the specialization level. Over the past one decade., the number of students enrolling for degrees in science has stagnated at the same level.

Indian S&T is at a crossroads. Globalization and the need for self-reliance, apparently contradictory in terms of their objectives, call for a realistic mix of policies. The myth of import of technology has been blasted loud and clear by unequivocal and frank warning by no less a person than Dr. A.P.J. Abdul Kalam and a few other scientists. Dr. Kalam pointed out that there is no such thing as a free lunch in the import of technology It we are not careful, we would often end up with less relevant, obsolete, eco—unfriendly technologies from developed countries, except in a few cases. We should accept the reluctance of developed countries to transfer technology in frontier areas and take up the challenge of developing our own technology in critical fields.

Unfortunately, liberalization has misled some people into believing that self-reliance has no relevance! Nothing could be more harmful to the interests of the country. In fact, at one time, the Confederation of the Indian Industry suggested the elimination of all restrictions on technology imports and foreign collaboration. While the removal cannot be 100 per cent, considerable liberalization has indeed taken place. Since the new Industrial Policy (1991), automatic approvals by the Reserve Bank for technology imports are allowed in cases pertaining to specific industries, where the total lump sum payment does not exceed Rs. 1 crore and the royalties on domestic sales and exports do not exceed five per cent and eight per cent, respectively. In 1994, for instance, 340 out of 915 cases got automatic approval. Hidden behind the plea for a 100 per cent automatic approval is a reluctance on the part of the industry to undertake any R&D so long as foreign products and processes are available and can be sold at high profit. In other words, this is described as "black box" approach, where one deals with technology as if it is a black box meant for trade only! It is an easy option but it cannot be adopted in the long-term interests of the country.

The truth is globalization is not a one-way street. Where there is expertise and resources, it becomes a two-way street, as for example, in India. Today, a wave of collaborative R&D is sweeping the world. Networking with premier R&D organizations around the world is becoming profitable. The evolution of a worldwide information network has made real time-management of production and marketing possible anywhere in the world. Leading companies from the US are coming to India since the country offers research facilities at low cost, a good science base, a fair legal framework and freedom and flexibility of operations. There is new breed of entrepreneurs in India who value quality and prompt delivery. With adequate intellectual property safeguards, more and more R&D firms are tying up with Indian counterparts, known for their world class research. For example, the National Chemical Laboratory(NCL),Pune, has licensed some of its patents to a Us firm. The Indian Institute of Chemical Technology, Hyderabad, has collaboration with DuPunt in agrochemical research. NCL is offering its services to China.

The Council of Scientific and Industrial Research (CSIR) has responded to this trend effectively. CSIR will soon have a "virtual" laboratory to monitor the data on what is being perfected or experimented in its laboratories. CSIR is no longer dependent entirely on government funds. It is supposed to earn up to 50 per cent of its experditure through commercial use of its products and processes. CSIR's external cash flow is expected to reach Rs. 145 crore during 1995-96. There is a suggestion from the private sector that the CSIR laboratories be converted into corporations and made the to compete in the market and sell their products and processes. However, many of the laboratories do not have effective competitors in the private sector.

About 75 per cent of the R&D expenditure is ment by the government on laboratories under its control. Only 25 per cent is met by the industry. However, the R&D expenditure by companies accounts for less than 0.1 per cent of their turnover. But the industry is slowly realizing the value of collaboration with research instiutions. For instance, three Indian Pharmaceutical companies have recently signed long-term agreements with government research laboratories for R&D in new drugs.

Industry is accused of not interacting closely with universities. It is a pity that the interaction between government laboratories and academic institutions has remained minimal. The Mashelkar Cpmmittee (1993) had made several specific recommendations for providing incentives to researchers and for exposing them to the international scientific community.

The Ninth Plan approach paper has indicated that emphasis would be made on networking between the research institutions/nationl laboratories both for development and marketing of technology. In order to achieve these objectives, the existing S&T infrastructure will be modernised through major investment by industry. Efforts would alsobe made to dispense with hierarchical bureucracy in the R&D institutions adequate delegation of powers, according to the approach paper.

Initiatives from Academic Bodies: Some initiatives from academic institutions are noteworthy. The Indian Institute of Science, Bangalore, is setting up special research cells for dealing with wpecific industrial problems in areas such as telecommunication, food processing, software engineering and drug design. The IIT, Chennai has set up a Center for Industrial Consultancy and Sponsored Research.

And Miles to Go: One test of technological excellence is the number of patents sealed in critical areas. A survey (1994) of the National Council for Applied Econmic Research of scientists working in Central government laboratories showec that the average number of patents applid for a scientist wa 0.13 and the patents obtained was 0.09. In terms of technology, the perceived gaps between the status quo and the state-of-the-art technology is 15-20 years in the paper industry, 10-15 years in cement, 10 years in polymers and 5-10 years in the paint industry. In specific cases, the gap would have since narrowed but the figures indicate the long road ahead in catching up with the state-of-the-art technology.

Addressing the Problem: Several initiatives have been taken to address the problem of enhancing the level of technology. The Technology Development Fund (TDF), created in 1994-95 to be financed from the five per cent cess on imported technologies through collaboration is expected to procure around Rs. 100 crore for the Department of Science and Technology. The TDF is expected to promote indigenous technology, especially in the small-scale sector. A Technology Development Board has been set up to assist in the use of the TDF. The approach paper says that besides continuing the initiatives taken during 1996-97, a Corpus Fund for financing research projects in frontier areas of scinece by distinguished scientists of any age, will be created. Efforts would also be made during the Ninth Plan to generate maximum resources for R&D from the production and service sectors.

Another initiative is the setting up of mission mode projects such as the one on fly-ash disposal and utilization. Yet another idea being tried is the location of clusters of industries (e.g. leather and jute) and supporting them with better facilities such as housing and health care.

However, the scheme offering tax deduction for sponsored research has not taken off in a big way. Only a few industries have responded to the broadcasting of 125 per cent weighted tax deduction for sponsored research in a national laboratory. This shows that the industry cannot be motivated by limited tax cuts alone. Market-driven demand seems to be a better incentive.

— The financial sector has a vital role in promoting efficiency and growth. It intermediates the flow of funds from those who want to save a part of their income to those who want to invest in productive assets. The efficiency of intermediation depends on the width, depth and diversity of the financial system. Till about two decades ago, a large part of household savings was either invested directly in physical assets, or put in bank deposits and Government small saving schemes. It is only since the late eighties that the equity market has started to play a role in this intermediation process. Other markets and short-term money markets, remain relatively segmented and underdeveloped. In recent decades, the Government and its subsidiary institutions and agencies, have had an overwhelming and all encompassing role. This has played a part in slowing the evolution and development of thse markets. The extensive system of controls, rules, regulations and procedures, directly or indirectly affects the development of these markets. We need to clear this web in the interest of both savers and those who invest in productive assets. Tax deductions and exemptions cannot be a substitute for reforms of policy and procedures. they can, however, create further distortions.

— The two most serious problems in the financial system are the lack of flexibility in intermediary behaviour and the segmentation of various markets and sets of financial intermediaries. Well developed markets are interconnected; demand-supply imabalances in one market overflow into related markets thereby dampening shocks and disturbances. This inter-connection also ensures that interest rates and returns in any market, reflect the broad demand-supply conditions in the overall market for savings. A rise in the demand for funds for investment, above the existing flow of funds from savings, leads to a rise in the interest rate or rate of return in all markets. The time lag may differ from market to market depending on economic factors. Conversely, a decline in demand for funds for investment below saving, leads to a fall in interest rates across the board. This does not happen in segmented markets. Adjustment in interest rates is also delayed by the slow speed of response of intermediaries and their lack of flexibility. Because of the historical role of the government and its subsidiary organisations in controlling and directing all financial activity, the autonomy and flexibility if intermediaries was greatly circumscribed. Consequently, adjustment to demand-supply imbalance in each segment was also very slow. Over the last five years a series of reforms. The widening and acceleration of reforms will increase the flexibility and responsiveness of the intermediaries and promote integration.

— The anuual (point-to-point) inflation rate in the first half of the currint financial year (April-September) ranged between a low of 4.2 per cent to a high of 6.6 per cent. The price rise of this magnitude could be regarded as modest given the hefty increase of 18 per cent in the administered prices of petrolium products in early July, 1996. Even in the next two months October-November 1996, the annual price rise was still below 7 per cent. However, there was a clear indication of inflationary pressures resurfacing due to the persistant rise in the prices of many of the agricultural commodities—mainly foodgrains—right from the middle of current financial year. By the end of December 1996, the annual inflation rate had crossed 7 per cent. The normal seasonal decline in the post-harvest period generally seen during November-December did not happen this year and hence the uptrend in prices was unabated in the third quarter of 1996-97. The containment of inflationary pressures in 1996-97. The containment of inflationary pressures in 1997-98 will require prudent fiscal and monetary policies and appropriate supply side policy measures to control price increases in primary articles.

— During the last financila year 1995-96, sanctions of financial assistance by development finance institutions recorded a growth rate of 18.5 per cent, while disbursements grew by 17.4 per cent. For investment institutions, the financial assistance sanctioned and disbursed declined by 31.4 per cent and 6.0 per cent, respectively, because of sluggish capital market conditions. During the first nine months of the current fiancial year (April-December 1996), The all India financial institutions disbursed Rs. 26813 crore as against Rs. 23187 crore disbursed in April-December 1995, implying an annual growth rate of 15.6 per cent. However, financial assistance sanctioned by them recorded a decline of 26.6 per cent. It appears that these institutions are mostly disbursing the pending sanctions of 1995-96. Development finance institutions disbursed Rs. 22256.9 crore as against Rs. 19088.1 crore in April-December 1995, the annual growth rate being 16.6 per cent. Assistance sanctioned by them, however, declined by 30 per cent. As UTI has become part of SEBI mutual fund discipline its loan sanctions and disbursements are being eliminated, as per SEBI guidelines relating to mutual funds.

— Most of the development finance institutions raised resources during the year through issue of bonds. Their interest rates have also become more or less market-based, in consonance with the ongoing liberalisation in the financial sector. Their interest rates increased in 1995-96 and in the first half of

1996-97, reflecting higher demand for funds on account of revival in real sector activities. Since October 1996, the minimum lending rate of DFIs, (excluding interest tax) has been reduced to 16.5 per cent from 17 per cent earlier.

— All India financial Institutions and the SEBI, led by IDBI, set up the North Eastern Development Finance corporation Ltd. (NEDFI) in the last financial year to cater exclusively to the financial needs of the industries in the North Eastern Region. The National Securities Depository Ltd. (NSDL), promoted by IDBI, UTI and National Stock Exchange of India (NSE) in December 1995, to maintain an electronic record of securities ownership details, started operations on November 8, 1996. IDBI got linked to the Society for Worldwide Interbank Fiancial Telecommunication (SWIFT) network tht processes and exchanges messages relating to overseas banking and foreign exchange business.

— In 1995.96, Small Industries Development Bank of India (SIDBI) set up a Technology Development and Modernisation Fund. This has an initial corpus of Rs. 200 crore. It will directly assist the SSIs in enhancing their export capabilities. SIDBI has also relaxed the norms under special schemes, to facilitate a greater flow of funds to industrially backward areas. It has widened the scope of the National Equity Fund and extended it to cover the whole country except for metropolitan cities. ICICI expanded its fee-based corporate advisory services to facilitate the creation of better projects and improvement in business environment. It initiated efforts in areas such as public sector restructuring and infrastructure projects. Industrial Reconstruction Bank India (IRB) has moved into business oriented activities from simple revival of sick units and also expanded its merchant banking activities. The Industrial Reconstruction Bank (Transfer of Under takings and Repeal) Ordinance, 1997 with a view to converting IRBI into a company under Companies Act, 1956, and transforming it into a full fledged financial institution.

Establishment Division is the nerve centre for the entire gamut of the service conditions of the Central Government employees having financial content. These activities are, therefore, spread over a vast spectrum of their service conditions right from the date of appointment to the date of retirement. Basically, these include revision/prescription of pay scales, fixation of pay and various allowances. The proposals received from various ministers/departments of the Government of India seeking calrification in regard to revision of pay scales, prescription of pay scales, increments, deputation allowance and cadre review of various categories of posts are examined in this Ministry keeping in view the equity and comparable relativities and duties. During 1994-95, 5th Central Pay Commission has been set up to review and make recommendation on the emoluments structure and service conditions, having financial bearing, of the Central Government employees.

Plan finance

Plan Finance-I Division handles matters relating to finances and plan outlays of states. It releases Central assistance to states for their Annual Plans (including for externally aided projects), Hill Areas Development Programme, Border Area Development Programme, Plan and Non-Plan revenue deficit grants and Centre's share to the Calamity Relief Fund (CRF) of the States. For 1994-95, the revised estimates of Central assistance to states for their Annual Plans amounted to Rs. 16,543.37 crore consisting of normal Central assistance-Rs. 10,914.97

crore, Special Central Assistance Rs. 973.00 crore, Special Plan Loan-Rs. 630.00 crore, Additional Central assistance for externally aided and other projects-Rs. 3,540.40 crore and Special Central Assistance for Hill Areas-Rs. 320.00 crore and Special Central Assistance for Border and Other Special Areas-Rs. 165.00 crore.

Against this, Rs. 16,599.71 crore was actually released to the states during 1994-95 on the basis of the provisional expenditure details furnished by them. Further, Plan and Non-Plan revenue deficit grants of Rs. 2,679.97 crore and Rs. 1,088.63 crore respectively and Centre's share of Rs. 462.64 crore to the Calamity Relief Fund of the states were also released to them. In addition, a grant of Rs. 17.95 crore was also released to Madhya Pradesh during 1994-95 for Bhopal Gas Tragedy Action Plan.

Plan Finance II Division deals with maters relating to the Central Plan. These cover the estimates of resources for Central Plan including internal and extra budgetary resources, Plan outlays of different ministries/ departments of the Central Government, appraisal of Plan projects/schemes before they are submitted to Public Investment Board (PIB)/Expenditure Finance Committee (EFC) etc. Plan Finance II is also the Secretariat of the PIB.

The PIB considers investment proposals of the Central Government ministries in regard to their public sector undertakings. Under the existing guidelines, central sector projects costing Rs. 50 crore and above are considered by PIB. Secretary (Expenditure) is the Chairman of the PIB and Joint Secretary (Plan Finance II) acts as the Secretary to the Board. During the period between 1 January and 31 December 1994, 11 meetings of PIB were held and 30 projects with a total capital cost of Rs. 11,404.51 crore were recommended for approval.

Estimation of internal and extra budgetary resource for financing the Annual Plan of the central public sector undertakings is an important activity of this Division. Recently, GOM was constituted under the Chairmanship of Finance Minister to review the proposals of sick PSUs for capital restructuring. Plan Finance II Division is mainly responsible to examine these proposals.

Under the Constitution, a Finance Commission is to be constituted every fifth year or at such earlier time as the President considers necessary to make recommendations to the President as to (i) the distribution between the Union and the states of the net proceeds of taxes which are to be, or may be, divided between them and the allocation between the states of the respective share of such proceeds; (ii) the principles which should govern the grants-in-aid of the revenues of the states in need of such assistance out of the Commission by the President in the interest of sound finance. The recommendations of the * Commission together with an explanatory memorandum as to the action taken thereon are laid before each House of Parliament. Ten Finance Commissions have been consituted since the commencement of the Constitution.

The Tenth Finance Commission constituted in pursuance of Article 280 of the Constitution by the Presidential Order dated 15 June 1992 submitted its report for the period 1995-2000 on 26 November 1994. Government accepted the recommendations of the Commission regarding devolution of Income-tax, Union excise duties, additional duties of excise in lieu of sales tax, grants in lieu of tax on railway passenger fares, grants-in-aid to cover non-plan gap on revenue account, financing of relief expenditure, grants for upgradation and special problems, grants for local bodies and debt relief. The report along with an explanatory menorandum on the action taken on the recommendations contained therein was placed on the table of each of the House of Parliament on 14 March 1995.

Finance Commission division implements the recommendations of the Finance Commission and also takes follow-up action on various observations of the Commission as contained in its report. Finance Commission Division also take advance action for setting up of the next Finance Commission.

Cost Accounts Branch of Ministry of Finance, Department of Expenditure renders professional assstance to different ministries and other agencies of Central Government in studies relating to cost aspects. This organisation was set up by the Government of India during World War II when defence contracts had to be placed on cost plus basis and the cost and price had to be vertified by an independent agency.

After Independence and with the growth of industrialisation, the role of the organisation changed and it became a body to render professional assistance to different ministries, committees and other agencies of the Government in cost, price fixation, reasonableness of prices charged investment appraisal, cost accounting system and other aspects. This Branch is manned by officers who are professionally qualified cost accounts and chartered accountants and they are members of the Indian Cost Accounts Service (ICAS), a Group 'A' Service constituted by Government of India in 1978. The needs of other ministries-Industry, Commerce, Petroleum and Natural Gas, Central Excise, etc., are also met by this Branch by posting ICAS officers to these ministries on participation basis.

This Branch is headed by Chief Adviser (Cost). He advises Department of Expenditure in the matters relating to the cadre administration of the Indian Cost

Accounts Service. The office of the Chief Adviser (Cost) also looks after the training requirements of the Service officers.

The Controller General of Accounts (CGA) is the apex accounting authority of the Central Government and exercises the powers of the President under Article 150 of the Constitution for prescribing the form of Accounts of the Union and state governments on the * Comptroller and Auditor General of India. The functions of the Controller General of Accounts (CGA) include, inter alia, the framing of rules, regulations etc., in the field of accounts and internal audit, the publication of accounts codes and manuals, issue of periodical instructions, cadre management of Civil Accounts personnel. The Junior Accounts Officers' Examination for Central ministries/departments, Cabinet Secretariat and union territories administrations e.g., Delhi, Andaman and Nicobar Islands, etc., is also conducted by the office of the Controller General of Accounts. It is also responsible for Government disbursements and banking arrangements of the various ministries/departments/ offices of the Government of India. The Controller General of Accounts has been closely studying and monitoring the extant system; significant improvements have been brought about in the reconciliation of cash balances of the Government with the RBI so far as civil ministries are concerned. These improvements are also being extended to other self-accounting Ministries of Railways, Defence and Posts and Telecommunications. A publication entitled "Accounts At A Glance" 1993-94 was brought out which gives broad and significant features of Government receipts and expenditure.

The office of the Controller General of Accounts is responsible for consolidation of accounts of Union Government which has been computerised. All the Principal Accounts Offices in Delhi have started transmitting floppies through the software IMPROVE. To speed up the work of consolidation of monthly accounts all the Principal Accounts Offices are being provided with a 386 DX machine along with dial up modern which would enable connectivity of these machines with the 486 machines housed in CGA office.

The Institute of Government Accounts and Finance was set up in February 1992 under the Controller General of Accounts as a Plan Project to impart in-service training on Government accounting, financial management, administrative and establishement matters to officials of the accounting organisation working in Central Government ministries/departments.

A Regional Training Centre has been set up at Calcutta and is fully functional, two more are also to be set up at Bombay and Madras. The Institute also conducted Induction Level training courses for newly recruited accountants. Orientation Training Programmes for the Drawing and Disbursing Officers and officers dealing with Finance and Budget in ministries were conducted by the Institute for some ofthe ministries.

The Management Training Programme on Preparation of Budget and Budgetary Exercises, Personnel Management, and Litigation and Vigilance Procedure for Controllers of Accounts and other officers were conducted in April and December 1994. The Institute also conducted training for a group of 25 officers of Government of Sri Lanka in May 1994 and five officials of Malawi in August 1994. Induction level orientation training on Government Accounts and Financial Management for Indian Civil Accounts Service Probationers after they complete professional training at National Institute of Financial Management has also been started and will continue to be a regular activity of the Institute.

The Central pension Accounting Office (CPAO), established as a unit of Ministry of Finance, commenced functioning w.e.f. 1 January 1990 for the purpose of administering primarily the scheme of payment of pension to Central Government civil pensioners by public sector banks. The Central Pension Accounting office is fully automated where the entire job right from the stage of receipt of correspondences to their final disposal is done on computer using roacle software having instant information retrieval facilities.

The Staff Inspection Unit (SIU) was set up in 1964 with the objective of securing economy in staff consistent with administrative efficiency and evolving performance standards and work norms. Where the SIU in the course of its work-measurement studies comes across procedures and methods whose revision or modification seems patently necessary and is likely to lead to economy in staff, it incorporates suitable recommendations in its reports. However, items requiring detailed methods study are brought to the notice of Department of Administrative Reforms and Public Grievances for further necessary action. SIU's reports are mandatory and have to be implemented in toto within a specified time frame.

The development so far in 1996—97 in the balance of payments, the Survey says, point to an easing of pressure on the current account and to buoyancy in capital inflows. The deficit on trade account in 1996—97 is expected to be lower than in the previous year, largely due to a sharp deceleration in the growth of non—petroleum imports. The improvement in trade deficit would be partly offset by anticipated decline in invisible receipts, reflecting an increase in payment for factor services and some decline in private transfers. The current account deficit is expected to decline from 1.7 per cent of GDP in 1995—96 to less than 1.4 per cent of GDP in 1996—97. Net capital inflows in 1996—97 are likely to be nearly three–fold over the previous year, largely because of buoyant inflows under non—resident deposits and foreign investment flows, including Euro—equities, and a sizable build—up of foreign exchange reserves. The foreign currency assets of the RBI rose by over US $ 2.8 billion from about US $ 17 billion at the end of March 1996, providing cover of about 5.5 months of imports.

The Survey says, exports during April—December period of 1996–97 grew only by 6.4 per cent as against 19.7 per cent during the previous three years. Among the significant reasons for the decline are slow down in world trade growth in 1996 (by about three percentage points). The latest trend in the growth rate of exports suggests that the initial impact of trade liberalisation is petering out and the trade flows are reverting to their normal trend determined by world demand and domestic activity. Despite the export slow down, self reliance as measured b;y the coverage of imports by exports, has risen by 88.2 per cent in April–December 1996 from 86.7 during 1995—96.

On the capital account, foreign investment continued to dominate capital fows. Total foreign investment (direct plus portfolio) during April–December 1996 surged to over US $ 4 billion, which is more than 50 per cent higher than in the corresponding period of 1995–96. This revival followed a modest decline in such investment flows from US $ 4.9 billion in 1994–95 to US $ 4.3 billion in 1995—96, mainly due to a sharp fall in the issue of Euro—equities. Foreign direct investment flows were US $ 2.1 billion in 1995—96. During April—December 1996. FDI flows were US $ 1.5 billion in the corresponding period of the previous year. Portfolio investment, comprising investment by FIIs and Euro—equities, doubled to over US $ 1.1 billion in the corresponding months of 1995—96.

India's external debt declined from US $ 99.0 billion at end—March 1995 to 92.2 billion at the end of March 1996. The downsizing of external debt resulted in a decline in debt–to–GDP ratio. The share of concessional debt in total debt remains stable at about 45.5 per cent. The share of short–term debt was 5.5 per cent at end–March 1996 and is low by international standards.

The survey does not provide current estimates of either poverty or employment generation, saying that the methodology of estimation is currently under the review of the Planning Commission. However, it says the government has accorded high priority to poverty alleviation programmes through an increase in the Central Plan allocations for social sectors and poverty alleviaton theweaker sections, specially scheduled castes and scheduled tribes and women have been given importance in special programmes of poverty alleviation and employment as well as in several other programmes. The Public Distribution System has also been streamlined recently in order to target the poorer sections of the population.

As outlined in the Update of the Economic Survey, fiscal deficit, reliable economic infrastructure services and broad–based employment—generating growth remain the key challenges for ecomomic policy. About fiscal deficit, as the Survey itself puts it "the normally difficult task of expenditure management will be accentuated in the coming years by the challenge of accommodating the recommendations of the Fifth Central Pay Commission." Further, as it says "the responsibility for fiscal consolidation and prudence does not rest with the Central Government alone."

About the infrastructure sector, as the Survey rightly puts it, the crux of the problem is of heavy investment. Both for infrastructure and other investment requirements of the economy, the country would need an inflow of foreign direct investment of US $ 10 billion per year as against US $ 2 to 3 billion currently. The Survey rightly exhorts al concerned to "learn from the pragmatic nationalism of China which received around US $ 40 billion of investment in 1996. We must also learn from the flexibility and speed of Indonesia, which modified its policies rapidly in response to perceived competition from China and India, to double foreign investment inflows between 1994 and 1996."

About poverty alleviaton, as the Survey puts it for the vast majority of the people it would have to be through job opportunities stemming through labour intensive Growth. For those at the margins of a market driven economy "the effective provision of minimum social services and special programmes for employment and poverty alleviation, fulfil an essential need." The basic goal, as the Survey puts it "should be to enhance sustainable benefits to the poorest segments of the society, while reducing administrative duplication and wastage and minimising well—known leakages."

Investment in infrastructure is to be stepped up from the present 3.5%-4% of the GDP to around $ 200 billion (Rs.7,00,000 crore) over the next five years. The Government is taking steps to boost both domestic and foreign investment so as to achieve the target of 12% annual industrial growth and 7% annual GDP growth. The Foreign Investment Promoton Board has been recast to make it a more effective and credible instrument to promote foreign investment in India, through adoption of greater transparency in rules and regulations as well as in the process of award of contracts. Complementary financial sector reforms are being made to ensure that enhanced domestic and foreign funds flow into this and other critical sectors. The response of the entrepreneurs to the policy initiatives has been very encouraging.

The data on foreign collaborations also indicates a strong and positive response to the structural reform measures. The Foreign Investment Promotion Council (FIPC) has been constituted to attract more foreign investment and to achieve the targeted FDI of US $ 10 billion by preparing project reports in selected thrust areas. The FIPC will also determine the exact snags in project implementation so that commencement of production is not unduly delayed.

The indicates that the overall investment in the corporate sector (the summation of Internal Savings, Assistance Disbursed, Capital Raised, and Capital Transfers from Abroad) is much higher than what has been indicated. There might be some double counting because the share premium which has been included in the amount raised from the primary market may also get included as the internal accruals of the corporate sector. Even after the suitable adjustments are made to avoid this double counting, it is likely that overall investment levels from 1992-93 onwards are much higher.

Overall employment in the SSI sector has been steadily increasing. In the ASI factory sector, employment after remaining virtually stagnant for over 10 years since 1980, recorded a growth of 6.2 per cent in 1992-93, the first year after the initiation of the reforms process. This suggests possible reorientation of the structure of production.

Though firm estimates of additional employment generated due to implementation of the IEMs filed or LOIs issued in the post policy period are not availabile, it is understood that nearly 20% of these intentions have actually been implemented and another 20% in different stages of implementation. Additional direct employment likely to be generated by these units would be over 1.7 to 2.0 million persons. Since IEMs/LOIs relate to units which employ more than 50 persons, net additional direct employment that would be generated with their implementation indicate an increase of over 20% to the total employment in respect of this sector.

The grosss profits of public sector enterprises have shown an increase of 21.3% compared to last year. Considering the fact that input costs and salaries and wages have increased by 2033 crore over the previous years, this growth in gross profits is impressive. The profit before tax and net profits have increased by 47.3% and 58.8% respectively over the last year.

The development of world class infrastructure insectors like power, transport and communication is critical for sustained industrial recovery. The Government is already considering extensive application of the market mechanism in these sectors through deregulation of production and distribution.

Foreign investment in these sectors is also being encouraged. In the power sector the policy package for private participation includes reduction of import duties, a five year tax holiday for new power projects and a 16% return on equity. New initiatives have also been considered in the mining sector to promote modernisation and investment.

For infrastructural development, Infrastructure Development Finance Corporation with an authorised capital of Rs. 5000 crore is being set up to act as a direct lender, refinancing agency and provider of financial guarantees. Income of any fund dedicated to infrastructure has been freed from tax. Plan outlay to infrastructure sectors has been increased. To step up investment in infrastructure, a levy of 2% as special customs duty on all imports except those that [illegible] a nil rate of duty or are imported at nil [illegible] for export production has also been proposed. Tax concessions have also been extended to infrastructure sector.

While it may be difficult to indicate the industry specific reasons, three factors which have significantly affected the growth rates are:

— The power sector has been behaving erratically and overall growth in April-August was only 2.1 per cent. In fact deceleration in the electricity growth rates is being witnessed since October, 1995.

— In 1995-96 industry was facing a liquidity crunch. To improve the liquidity situation, Reserve Bank revised the CRR twice from 14% to 12%. However, due to the continued pre-emption of funds advances by the Government, easing of liquidity does not seem to have positively favoured the non Government sector.

— Along with the availability of funds there has also been increase in their cost. The overall lending rate of the institutions and commercial banks are in the range of 18 to 20%. With the inflation rate currently running at around 6%, the nominal interest rate for industry at 18 to 20% makes effective real interest rate of 12% to 14% which are perceived very high. The current interest rates are higher than the average return on capital employed which is reported to be around 18% for the corporate sector. This is infact resulting in withholding of investment by entrepreneurs. The sanction of term loans by the financial institutions has declined for the first time during April-July, 1996 by 21.8% compared to the same period in the previous year validating the fact that the investment intentions are being kept pending. IFCI data show further slide in sanctions in

The Government has gradually moved to borrow funds at market related rate of interest. The rate of interest on Gilt Securities, therefore, tend to become the bench-mark interest rate. While lending to the corporate sector and deciding the prime lending rates for such lending, the financial intermediary would require to add additional transaction and monitoring cost and the perceived risk in such transactoins. There are no precise estimates of these costs which financial intermidiaries will have to incorporate. However, the ceiling of non performance assets indicated by Reserve Bank of India provide us the likely bad debts in lending to the corporate sector. The transaction and monitoring cost of the corporate loan could roughly be taken as additional 10% markup. This makes the calculation of PLR which might subconsciously being followed by the financial intermediaries. According to this assessment, the minimum PLR for the financial intermediaries 15.8% to 16% for commercial banks and financial institutions. Since the bench mark rate is determined by Gilt Securities rates, there is little possibility of PLR coming down in the medium term given the risk averse nature of the financial intermidiaries in India.

The other possibility of interest rates coming down basically rests on excess supply of loanable funds. The information on the monetary variable upto 13th September, 1996 indicate that the Government's pre-emption from the market continues to exceed 100%. Government is withdrawing more than the total credit created by the commercial bank system. With shortfall in excise the custom collection and government's expenditure liabilities remaining fixed, the possibility of this pre-emption getting reduced is remote. In view of this the excess fund available with the commercial bank would continue to find an out-let in Government securities. This is evident from continuous increase in the holdings of Government securijties in excess of SLR stipulations. Even if Government reduces CRR and releases additional liquidity in the system, additional demand of funds by the Government being so high, almost insatiable, flow of funds to the corporate sector may not increase. Further any decrease in the interest rate of Gilt Securities if it is marginal, will not induce commercial banks and institutions to off load their surplus fund in the corporate sector because the perceived risk may be higher than the ratio of non performance assets being prescribed would indicate. An alternative risk perception scenario could be based on the ratio of outstanding commercial banks credit in sick/ weak industrial units which have been around 14% in 1990s. Given the risk averse nature of the financial intermediaries in India the risk perception is bound to be higher than that indicated by the non-performance asset ratio. In view of this and continued government's pre—emption of resources from market, in the medium term the possibility of interest rates coming down appears to be remote.

An estimate of all anticipated receipts and expenditure of the Union for the ensuing financial year is laid before the Parliament. This is known as 'Annual Financial Statements' or 'Budget' and covers Central Government's transactions of all Kinds, in and outside India, occuring during the preceding year, the year in which the statement is prepared as well as the ensuring year or the 'Budget Year' as it is known.

The presentation of Budget is followed by a general discussion on it in both Houses of Parliament. Estimates of expenditure from the Consolidated Fund of India are placed before the Lok Sabha in the form of 'Demands of Grants'. All withdrawals of money from the Consolidated Fund are thereafter authorised by an Appropriation Act passed by Parliament every year. Tax proposals of

Budget are embodied in a Bill which is passed as the 'Finance Act' of the year. Estimates of receipts and expenditure are similarly presented by state government's in their legislatures before the beginning of the financial year and legislative sanction for expenditure is secured through similar procedure.

Tax concession

However, municipalities looking to municipal bonds as a feasible option should not forget that their popularity abroad is due to their tax exemption status. For the most part, the bond holder in the US do not have to pay federal taxes on the interest and usually do not have to paystate or local taxes if the bond is issued in the state of his or her residence. A California resident would not have to pay state taxes on Califormia bonds, for instance, New York City obligations are TRIPLE TAXEXEMPT to gcity residents whose income is taxed at federal, state and local levels. However, in India it is debatable whether there is tax exemption from interest income for municipal bonds as there is no Constitutional backing for the tax exemption. There are strong opinions to make kthese bonds tax free initially to entice the investors. Government too in t;he recent budget has given positive signal for same tax benefit to the infrastructure sector.

From the investors' point of view the primary issue is redemption. For this there has to be an active secondary market for debt instruments. During the past few years debenture financing has been on rising trend inspite of poor secondary markeft conditions. Investors were more enthusiastic towards the dept issue as compared to equity offerings. Keeping in view this trend BSE and NSE had to start separate trading wing in, the debt instruments. Among all the stock exchanges in India, NSE seems to be the best bet as it is more popular for the debt instruments. OTCEI can be the other alternative for listing of municipal bonds due to its market facilities. However, OTCEI now a days is no body's baby. How far it will succeed in giving tje adequate return to investors of municipal bonds only the time will tell.

The availability of market intermediaries and faster listing arrangements hold the key to future success of municipal bondss. Even if all the above problems are set right the legal risk in the event of default remains to be clearly defined. Given the instability of octroi as a future revenue source debt servicing ability of the issue becomes a crucial issue considering the rates they would have to offer. Authorities seem to be silent about the investors who face default risk on account of non receipt of redemption amount from municipalities. Bankruptcy laws need amendment to cover such institutions. SEBI can think of Municipal Bond Insurance policies underwritten by private investors guaranteeing municipal bonds in the event of default. The insurance can be purchased either by the issuing government entity or the investor, it provides that bonds will be purchased from investors at par should default occur. Such insurance is available in the US from a number of large insurance companies, but a major portion is written by two organisations: American Municipal Bond Assurance Corporation (AM-BAC), a private corporation, and Municipal Bond Insurance Association (MBIA), a pool of private insurance.

Insured municipal bonds will enjoy the highest rating resulting in greater marketability and lower cost to the issuers. In such a situation, at least initially, undue emphasis of market to accept only top quality issues will have no importance. From the investor's stand point, however, their yield would be typically lower than similarly rated uninsured bonds as the cost of insurance will be passed on by the issuer to the investor. Setting up

Municipal Investment Trust (MIT) can be yet another alternative to minimize risk exposure of investor. These unit popular in the US. They buy municipal bonds and pass the tax-free income on to shareholders. Bonds in the trust's portfolio are normally held until maturity, unlike the constant trading of bonds in an open-ended municipal bond fund's portfolio. The trust offers diversification, professional management of the portfolio, and monthly interest, compared with the semi annual payments made by individual municipal bonds.

The issue of rating is yet another crucial issue to be addressed. Given the reputaion that municipalities enjoy coupled with the lack of commercial glamour of municipal projects, rating may be the only machanism to make such bonds attractive to investors. Rating agencies however will be making a fool of investors if they give higher rating to municipalities on account of highly depedent single revenue source, i.e. octroi. Let us see the present trend. 65% of ABC revenue comes from octroi. Bombay Municipal Corporation's annual income from octroi is Rs. 650 cr. with 20% increase every year. This means in the event of octroi being withdrawn corporation will not be credit worthy any more and debt service ratio would mount. Crisil however, was cautions to keep the ratings of ABC to investment grade despite the impressive financial structure. Further, keeping in view the accounting principles being followed by some of the municipal corporations there seems to be a problem [illegible] a rating. For example, according to one report August, 1996. principles followed the Municipal [illegible] Bombay do not confirm to any [illegible] Barring the financially [illegible] ntly meeting [illegible] receipt.

due to its own attached employees. It becomes difficult to make any financial assessment or debt service ratios on account or unreliable accounting systems being followed by municipalities. Hence for bringing the qualitative issue in the market it is desirable that the entire working of municipalities are overhauled. This should be both in terms of revenue earning capabilities as well as expenditure and price of service. It may also be prudent for municipalities to start experimenting with alternative mechanisms of increasing revenues for servicing debt okbligations and decreasing the credit risk. Some of the alternatives may be charging substantial property taxes (e.g. Kerala Mu;n;icipal Corporation), increasing user fees (e.g., Bombay Municipal Corporation) and using ad hoc appraisal methods especially where bonds are subscribed by institutional investors. Thus the success of municipal bonds has a long way to go. But if the impetus is given in the right direction the municipal bonds have a very big role to play in municipal financing.

Policies of the government

The Common Minimum Programme (CMP) provides a clear indication of the Government's commitment to accelerate the process of economic reforms and to address some areas of weakness that have emerged.

Among the major themes of the CMP are:

— An overarching commitment to growth with social justice.

— A growth target of 7 per cent year in the next 10 years.

— A commitment to fiscal prudence with the goal of reducing the fiscal deficit to below 4% of GDP.

— A commitment to strengthen anti-poverty programmes and target subsidies in favour of the poor.

— A commitment to increase investment in the social sectors.

— A commitment to continue the process of tax reform and bring about a phased reduction in customs duties.

— A commitment to decontroal and reform in the agricultural sector.

— A target of maintaining 12 per cent annual growth of industry.

— A target of $ 10 billion a year of foreign direct investment.

— A commitment to reform and restructuring public sector enterprises, including through disinvestment.

— A commitment to developing the infrastructure sectors through all modes of investment, public and private domestic and foreign.

The Government has moved swiftly to implement the agenda outlined in the CMP.

The programme of tax reform has been carried forward along the lines articulated by the Tax Reforms Commitee, import duties have been reduced for a wide range of products. The intension is to eventually move to duty rates comparable to those prevailing in other developing South-East Asian economies, the Modvat system of rebates of excise tax on imputs to the singly most important industrial sector in India, namely, textiles, has been extended, the surcharge on corporate taxation reduced by half and introduced Minimum Alternate Tax as a measure of broadening the base of taxation.

The Government is committed to fiscal prudence by reducing the fiscal deficit to 5 per cent of GDP for 1996-

97 as compared to 5.9 per cent in 1995-96 (Revised Estimates). A number of initiatives to deal with three critical areas of weakness in the economy are: agriculture, infrastructure and social sectors. In agriculture, the budget has made allocations for strengthening the capital base of the National Bank for Agricultural and Rural Development, the principal refinance institution in agricultural credit. It has also provided funds for re-capitalising Regional Rural Banks and has launched an important new initiative for private local area banks. Agricultural infrastructure will be strengthened through a large special allocation to finance completion of a number of irrigation schemes.

For infrastructure, a number of fiscal incentives are being provided in the budget. The tax holiday earlier provided for power, telecommunications and road transport has been extended to other infrastructure sectors such as water supply, sewerage and irrigation. It also exempts from income-tax the income of dedicated infrastructure funds which invest in equity and debt instruments of infrastructure companies. The existing income tax incentive available for long-term savings under Section 88 of the Income Tax Act has beden extened to include bonds issued by infrastructure companies or by financial institutions leading to infrastructure projects. The budget has also announced the formation of a new Infrastructure Development Finance Company (IDFC) which will fill some critical gaps in financing of commercially viable infrastructure projects. This institution could act as a direct lender, as a refinance institution, as a channel for multilateral funds and as a provider of various types of financial guarantees for infrastructure projects. The intention is that the IDFC will induce investors in India and abroad to make available long-term funds at the lowest market rates. The budget has alo provided resources for the National Highway Authority of India to help fund its operations.

In the social sectors, a number of schemes have been launched to strengthen the provision of basic minimum services and has generally expanded allocations for social services and anti-poverty programmes.

The Government welcomes foreign investment and has taken a number of concrete steps to achieve this objective. The Foreign Investment Promotion Board has been restructured to make the process of foreign investment approval speedier and more transparent. 350 foreign investment projects have been cleared involving a total foreign equity of US $ 4 billion. A new Foreign investment Promotion Council has been established aimed at reaching out to foreign investors and represent their concerns to the Government. The Government has announced that the list of 35 industries which are eligible for automatic approval of foreign investment upto 51 per cent of equity will be expanded in order to accelerate the approval process. The regulations governing foreign institutional investor have been amended to allow these investors to make equity investments in unlisted companies. Hitherto, they were limited to investing in listed companies only. The limit of investment of 5 per cent of total equity in a single company by an individual FII has been rasied to 10 per cent. The Securities and Exchange Board of India (SEBI) regulations are being amended to allow FIIs to set up 100 per cent debt funds to facilitate FII investment in corporate debt instruments. The guidelines for Euro issues have been liberalised to ease access of Indian companies to international capital markets.

In the area of capital markets, landmark legislation enabling the establishment of depositories for share trading has been passed during the Budget session of Parliament. The first depository is expected to become operational in November this year. Stronger guidelines have been issued for disclosure in the offer documents of primary issues and a number of other steps have been taken to strengthen investor protection. New guidelines have been brought out for mutual funds in general and for money market mutual funds in particular.

The process of financial sector reform has been continued on several fronts. Reserve requirements of banks have been reduced; many more public sector banks have reached capital adequacy norms set out several years ago; regulation of interest rates on bank deposits has been reduced so that they remain only on maturities upto one year; and more private sector banks have become operational. Interest rates charged on loans have been comletely deregulated for Regional Rural Banks to improve their financial viability. It has been decided to allow private sector local area banks to be set up which will operate in two or three districts. These banks will be subject to RBI regulations but will have lower initial capital requirements and will benefit from the interest rate deregulation extended to Regional Rural banks. The process of reforms in the banking sector has borne fruit in the form of significant reduction in non-performing asset of public sector banks and higher profits.

Non-Bank Financial Companies (NBFCs) which comply with the dual requirement of credit rating and prudential norms have been allowed freedom to fixed interest rates on deposits. At the same time, the reserve bank of India has imposed a ceiling on interest rates which can be offered by the mutual benefit financial companies (MBFCs) which do not meet the prudential standards set by RBI.

A number of steps have been taken to strengthen the market for Government securities including the issue of guidelines for primary dealers in Government securities. The first set of such dealers have begun operation. Following the announcement in the budget, legislation is being proposed to provide statutory backing to new, Insurance Regulatory Authority. Similarly, quick action has been taken to establish the Disinvestment Commission announced in the budget.

Traditionally in India municipalities used to operate within the frame work of laws enacted by the state legislature. Sources of raising money by municipal bodies used to be approved by the state legislature which in turn rested on the latter's degree of commitment to the principle of devolution. Article 243x of the Constitution specifically authorise the state legislation to entrust local bodies with powers and functions. Though 73rd and 74th Amendments to the Constitution no doubt stressed the importance of devolution of powers to municipal bodies. State legislature continued to be the resource base for municipalities. However, with the growing pace of urbanization, soaring cost of funds due to intermediaries, sluggish collecton on account of octroi and property taxes and decreased Central and State level capital receipt there had been a mismatch of supply of funds and demand for infrastructural facilities. Faced with a slow down in the economy and declline ingovernment grants there has been a sea change in borrowing mechanism of municipalities. Municipalities had no other opton except to break their shell and access the capital market for raising resources. Much of the inspiration for such rapid development in municipal financing in India comes from the US municipal bond markets where the volume of municipal debt outstanding at the end of 1995 stood at a staggering $ 1015 billion. This marks yet another attempt to reduce government's monopoly and a step towards private sector participation in the development of nfrastructural facilities. The trend setter in this area was Ahmedabad Municipal Corporation (AMC) planning to tap the market with an Rs. 100 crore bond issue. The issue has been rated by Crisil. Bombay Municipal

Corporation has been the second entrant in this field by submitting its proposal to crisil. Other municipalities that are planning to tap the market are Coimbatore in Tamil Nadu, surat and Rajkot in Gujarat municipalities of Madras, bangalore, Vijayawada, Nagpur and New bharatpur. However, each of them is playing safe and plans to enter the market oncethe response to AMC is kknown. This move has largely been facolitated by changes made to Article 243 of the Constitution empowering local bodies to function as autonomous institutions. Another factor has been the growing confidence of investors towards to bond market that prompted municipalities to make a grand entry into the bond market.

Municipal bonds are dept obligations issued by a State or local municipal entityl. The funds raised may support a government's general financial needs or may be spent by financing core urban infrastructural facilities like drinking water, sanitary system, road development, hospitals, etc. In general, municipal bonds are issued in form of general obligation bonds (GOBs) and revenue bonds (RBs).

If the Plan objectives and programmes are to be translated into reality, the close co-operation and co-ordination from the States is essential. The economic reform programmes which form a guide-post of the Central direction could succeed only if the States are sincere and committed to the cause. Much of the benefits of direct investment depends on the policy and initiative of the State governments. Reforms can receive greater acceptability only if poverty alleviation measures are implemented vigorously, which has to be done by the States. The development of infrastructure and social sector has ultimately to be implemented by the States.

We have already noted that a vital constraint of growth and development is unchecked population. The family welfare programmes and population control mechanism are in the hands of State governments. Statistics show that some States have advanced in the direction while others are lagging behind. The story of success or failure in this direction has been caused by the extent to which the States are sincere and devoted to the cause. The newly revamped public distribution system of the deva Gowda government has decided to supply 10 kg of food grains at half the PDS price to 60 million families below the poverty line "in order that nobody could complain about the step as the aim was to benefit the poor." It may be recalled that during the Food Ministers' conference at New Delhi in August 1996, the State Food Ministers refused to withdraw the PDS benefits from affluent classes and also to raise the price of ration items. Again, the identification of families below the poverty line lies with the State government. Though the Centre has asked the States to set up vigilance committees at the Panchayat level to supervise identification, the success of the scheme will largely depend on how sincere are the agencies entrusted with the responsibility, other things remaining the same.

In order to achieve the seven minimum basic services in particular and the rural development schemes in general, the Centre has instructed the States to constitute vigilance and monitoring committees at the block, district and State levels for the effective implementation of rural development programmes across the country. The government has taken action to strengthen the District Rural Development Agencies (DRDAs) with adequate technical staff at various levels. These are important agencies for poverty alleviation programmes. Thus, at every level of plan efforts, success will depend chiefly on the States' implementation level.

Estimates committees recommendations

It is pertinent here to recall certain observations made by the Lok Sabha Estimates Committee of Parliament in 1992-93. The 19th Report may well be described as a monumental monogram on Defence management and Policy, besides force levels and manpower.

The Committee have felt that the existing statement on defence policy which is, to defend territorial integrity of the country, is a needless over simplification. They have also expressed dismay over the fact that suddenly emerging situations like Gulf War of 1990 should have thrown country's defence planning into dissarray or that country should have fought four wars and launched armed operations in and at the request of neighbouring countries without a clearly articulated and integrated defence policy. The Committee has therefore stressed upon the need for a clear and comprehensive defence policy based on a viably national security doctrine. In the same context the Committee have recommended review and rationalisation of the Officials Secret Act to facilitate a more meaningful debate on national security affairs.

The Committee have suggested revival of dormant national security council for holistic direction of national security affairs at the highest level. From this perspective the Committee have desired that the defence policy makers should take a greater note of emerging threat to the country from air and sea.

With a view to stabilising defence plan expenditure the Committee have called for studying the feasibility of making the defence sector allocation for the entire plan unalterable. This the Committee feel will make defence planning exercise more realistic by co-relating allocation of resources to the task entrusted to the defence services. Commenting on the efficiency of decision making process in the Ministry of Defence, the Committee have observed that often proposals floated for fulfilling the task entrusted to defence services are subjected to such prolonged process of scrutiny and series of clearance that it assumes the form of a hurdle race and in the bargain the services end up with a relatively larger share of anxiety. To mitigate ths situation the Committee have highlighted the need to reform the decision making process in the Ministry of Defence. To this end, they have called for greater powers to be delegated to the three Chief of Staff.

Despite the Estimates Committee's emphatic recommemdations, the Government has been implementing them in a piecemeal manner with the result that many essential items are still to be cleared for procurement by the defence services. This has its cascading effect on defence preparedness due to a lack of appreciation of perspective planning by the nodal Ministr. Infact, the three services have a Director General for Defence Planning but their recommendations of a long term nature have had little effect on decision makers.

Therefore, the need is to change track in the same manner as government did in the sectors of the economy. Another major imperative is to take out the Defence Budget from the non-plan category and bring it within the overall planning process. This is immensely desirable in order to make the Defence Sector Undertakings enter into diversified manufacture or civilian sector also. The Current year's Defence Budget is of the order of Rs. 27,798 crore as against Rs. 26,879 crore last year. The allocaton for present year include a capital outlay of Rs. 8979 crore on all the three services. Often there is a debate on this capital segment. But in the absence of detailed expenditure Budget documents such discussion becomes an exercise in futility.

A major part of this outlay is committed expenditure on ongoing projects including procurement and construction but does not provide for any new acquisitions sought by any of the services. This is a lacuna and has to be covered up by a projected allocation offunds as and when required for additions to the defence services arsenal. Otherwise there is general demoralisation in the armed services which feel that they are not getting their deserved priority, although the case may be otherwise.

India has a large Army, the fifth biggest in the world. The Navy and Air Force too have their unique position figuring among the top five or six. But strange to say there is a very big communication gap between the Armed Forces and the public and what hits the eye most is the denial of access to the media to the state of defence preparedness

The Press Council of India has admirably defined the role of the press in coverage of defence related matters in its Report (1994) calling for more openness in defence coverage. The Council said the media has an "adversarial role" to the extent that it questions authority, all authority, to look at the otherside. This must be understood and a relationship of creative tension accepted as a democratic necessity. For the rest, they are partners in trying to build a better society".

One must however congratulate the Army Chief General Shankar Roy Choudhary for his frank and forthright advise to his troops and officers to develop media interaction modes and use it as a "force multiplier and not as a force degrader". Infact, this is among the Ten Commandments prepared by the Army Headquarters as advice to troops engaged in low intensity conflict situations. This thus shows the appreciation of the role of the media in giving a boost to defence preparedness in all its magnitude but sadly it remains to be implemented in letter and spirit.

No doubt a good beginning has been made recently by the Army Training Command (ARTRAC) which has organised a number of inter-media Seminars at a number of locations but the feedback has not been as fruitful as it should be. At least the consolation is that after a long time the three services are coming to realise that the print and electronic media are weighty partners in the process of defence preparedness and policy making.

To conclude, it must be understood that the nature of modern warfare is such that it involves the whole nation. Of course Defence Forces play a key role but since war or any external threat requires total mobilisation in a democracy, maximum transparency alone can assure co-operation on the part of the people in every respect.

The balance of payments adjustment in the aftermath of the 1991 crisis has been remarkably smmoth. The adjustment was made possible mainly because of the dynamic growth in exports and large foreign investment flows. International prices of petroleum were also favourable for most part of the period. The balance of payments outlook in the medium term will depend critically on several factors. First of all, as reiterated in earlier Economic Surveys, it is absolutely imperative of sustain rapid export growth to assure external sector viability. Tremendous efforts would be required to ensure this on an increasing base of exports and in the context of a difficult international trading environment. Second, taking into account the importance of POL in the total import bill and the uncertainty surrounding the future movement of oil prices, concerted efforts on the demand and the supply sides are required to contain the POL import bill at manageable levels. The rapid rise in POL consumption in recent years is a matter of concern.

The growth of consumption of petroleum products will have to be contained through an appropriate pricing policy, and by effecting energy efficiency in the use of petroleum products in the transport and other sectors of the economy which are major users of petroleum. On the supply side, concerted efforts are required to increase domestic production of crude oil and augment refining capacity. The saving on POL imports will allow sufficient room for imports of raw materials, components and capital goods consistent with the requirements of a growing economy without undue pressure on the balance of payments.

Earnings from tourism have been a mojor component of invisibles. Tourism industry, apart from being a major foreign exchange earner, contributes substantially to sustainable human development, including poverty alleviation, employment generation, environmental regeneration and advancement of women. The sector also· helps to pressure and promote handicrafts, arts and the cultural heritage of the country. Inadequate infrastructure has become the main impediment to the accelarated growth of tourism in India. In fact, there is an acute shortage of approved accommodation, transport and other tourism facilities in all the metro cities and other major tourist centers. The Department of Tourism has initiated several measures for attracting large scale private investment in the tourism sector, including declaration of tourism as a priority sector for foreign investment provision of incentives and setting up of an investment facilities cell to provide information about investment opportunities and to facilitate investment. The State/Union Territory Governments are also offering a number of financial and fiscal incentives to tourism industries. These efforts are to be sustained an intensified to make India na all-season attractive tourist destination in the world.

The importance of foreign investment, as a major source of capital flows for sustaining a high current account deficit without imposing an excessive burden on the external debt management ability, has been described amply in the earlier sections. In order to strengthen the balance of payments and garner more foreign savings to meet the investment needs of the economy, India needs to maintain a welcoming stance towards direct foreign investment and continue to clarify policies in areas where there may be ambiguities.

Borrowings under external assistance constitute the most desirable form of debt creating capital flows, because of their favourable terms in regard to period of maturity and interest rates, conferring significant benefit in the form of concessionality. Given the international aid environment, though India may have reached a stage of graduating from being eligible for large flows as in the past, the substantial build-up of aid in the pipeline offers enormous scope for increasing the level of disbursements from the commitments secured so far. India should also take advantage of the offer of currency choice for existing IBRD currency pool loans and the offer of a broad range of terms for new IBRD loan commitments. This provides the borrowers flexibility to select terms that are consistent with their debt management strategy and suited for their debt servicing capability.

Even with the optimistic outlook for foreign investment and sustaining the normal trends in other traditional sources of capital flows, there will still be a large uncovered gap between domestic savings and investment requirements, if the economy were to grow at a sustained rate of about 7 per cent per annum. This will imply that borrowings on commercial terms will be inescapable. However, such borrowings should be consistent with the achievement of a sustainable balance of payments position over the medium and long term.

Capital account convertibility entails some risk of capital flight and possible macroeconomic instability arising from movements of short-term, cross-border capital flows. Such risks and vulnerability remain contained as long as prudent macroeconomic policies are followed and the financial system is sound and flexible to rapidly adapt to changing situations. Thus, a reduction in fiscal deficit, moderation in inflation, a sustained dynamic export performance, strengthening of domestic financial institutions, and a further build-up of foreign exchange reserves are some of the preconditions for a move towards capital account convertibility. It should also be recognized that capital account convertibility indirectly imposes discipline on the conduct of policies by increasing the cost associated with policy failures. However, strengthening the prudential supervision of financial institutions, and putting in place appropriate institutional arrangements for speedy foreign exchange and payments clearing systems constitute major elements in ensuring a smooth transition to full convertibility.

The investment in Research and Development. (R & D) has increased from a paltry Rs. 20 crore in the First Five Year Plan. Presently there are 214 universities, 400 national laboratories and 1300 in-house R & D centres in the industrial sector. Several Science & Technology departments have been set up in the areas of environment, non-conventional energy resources, bio-technology, ocean development, industrial research, space, atomic energy, defence, health, agriculture and electronics.

Identification and promotion of priority areas in R & D is done by Science an Engineering Research Council (SERC) set up under the Department of Science & Technology (DST). DST supports 12 autonomous research insitutions as well, for furthering research work in several discipline. Technology Information, Forecasting and Assessment Council (TIFAC) has been set up for generating technology forecasting and technology assessment documents and enabling a technology information system that is interactive and nationally accessible.

Industrial research in several diverse fields of scientific activity is being undertaken through a network of 40 laboratories and 81 field stations set up by the Council for Scientific and Industrial Research (CSIR). In the field of bio-technology, more than 24 specialised R & D centres have been developed for pursuing state-of-the-art research. Identical efforts for promoting new avenues of research are being undertaken in the field of ocean development as well.

The Union Budget for 1996-97 has taken various measures to promote R & D facilities. A matching one time grant has been awarded to CSIR and the Indian Council of Agricultural Research (ICAR) for modernisation of laboratories and institutes. The Technology Development and Application Fund created in 1995-96 has been proposed to be strengthened by Rs. 30 crore. A Five Year Tax Holiday under Section 80-IA of the Income Tax Act has been allowed to companies exclusively create for participation in R & D activities. The existing procedure for awarding weighted deduction under Section 35(2AA) of the Income Tax Act on sums paid for scientific research to a National Laboratory or a University or an IIT has been amended, by deleting the condition of approval by an outside body. In order to encourage R & D efforts, goods developed and patented in India and concurrently in specified countries have been exempted from levy of excise duty for a period of 3 years. The exemption procedure for customs duty on import of equipment and consumables for R & D institutions has been rationalised as well.

The following five committees of the National Development Council were constituted to go into some of the critical areas of development: (i) Committee on Austerity, (ii) Committee on Population, (iii) Committee on Employment, (iv) Committee on Micro-Level Planning; and (v) Committee on Literacy.

The meeting of the National Development Council held on 5 April 1993 considered the report of the NDC Committee on Austerity. The Council generally endorsed the recommendations of the report of the Committee. It was also decided to set up a NDC Committee on Power. Accordingly, NDC Committee on Power under the Chairmanship of Chief Minister, Maharashtra, was constituted to examine measures to make state electricity boards economically viable by recasting tariffs, improving efficiency and considering delinking of distribution from generation.

A Committee headed by Deputy Chairman, Planning Commission was constituted to evolve a suitable formula for distribution of Central assistance to Non-special Category States. The suggestions made by the Committee were discussed by the NDC in its meeting on 23-24 December 1991, wherein a consensus emerged and a revised formula evolved which was made the basis for allocation of Central Plan assistance to the states for the Eighth Plan. Under the criterion of the progress in respect of national objectives, the approved formula highlights four objectives, viz., (a) population control and maternal and child health; (b) universalisation of primary education; (c) on-time completion of externally aided projects; and (d) land reforms.

Achievements

During the 43 year period (1950-51 to 1993-94), Net National Product (NNP) at factor cost at 1980-81 prices increased from 40,454 crore to Rs. 2,02,670 crore implying compound growth rate of 3.8 per cent per annum. Advance estimates of GDP for 1994-95 project a growth rate of 5.3 per cent over 1993-94. During the First Five year Plan (1951-56), national income increased by 3.6 per annum. In the Second Five Year Plan (1956-61), however, the growth rate actually achieved was four per cent annum against the target of 4.5 per cent per annum.

In the Third Plan (1961-66), there was a sharp decline in the growth rate at 2.3 per cent per annum and fell well short of the target at 5.6 per cent per annum. This was primarily due to the steep fall in agricultural production and consequent decline in NNP at factor cost of 4.65 per cent in the last year of the Third Plan. However, during the subsequent three Annual Plans, the economy picked up and the growth rate during 1965-69 was 3.7 per cent per annum. Fourth Five year Plan (1969-74), the growth rate target was fixed at 5.7 per cent in terms of NDP at factor cost. However, the actual growth rate achieved was only 3.3 per cent per annum.

The economy took an up-turn during the Fifth Five Year Plan (1974-79). The growth rate fixed in terms of GDP at factor cost of 4.4 per cent per annum was over-achieved at 4.8 per cent annum for the Fifth Five Year Plan. In 1979-80, however, the economy faced a severe drought resulting in the decline of GDP at factor cost by 5.2 per cent over the previous year. The economy bounced back on the track during the Sixth Plan (1980-85) period when the rate of growth in GDP at factor cost at 5.6 per cent per annum surpassed the target of 5.2 per cent per annum. Despite successive drought condistions during the first three years of the Seventh Plan (1985-90), the economy has fared exceptionally well. The growth rate achieved during Deventh Plan period was six per cent per annum and this surpassed the target of five per cent per annum in GDP at factor cost for the Seventh Plan.

During 1991-92, the country faced a severe fiscal crisis and the balance of payment situation became so critical that exceptional measures had to be restored to. While the growth momentum enabled an increase in GDP by 5.4 per cent in 1990-91, the growth in 1991-92 was only 0.9 per cent. In 1992-93 the economy registered the growth of 4.3 per cent and this had been mainly due to high growth in agriculture and improvement in sectors of trade, hotel and restaurants, transport by other means, storage, communication and the public administration and defence, despite railways and banking and insurance sectors registering a decelerated growth. The GDP from agriculture and allied sectors recorded a growth of 5.1 per cent in 1992-93 as compared to 2.3 per cent in 1991-92.

Important policy reforms had been made during June 1991 towards liberalisation and structural adjustment of the economy. These measures have started showing results. The annual rate of inflation as measured by the wholesale price index declined from 13.6 per cent at the end of 1991-92 to seven per cent in 1992-93. The inflation rate stood at 10.8 per cent in 1993-94. The Eighth Plan has targeted for a GDP growth of 5.6 per cent per year, a substantial reduction in the average annual inflation rate, about five per cent and the average current account deficit of about 1.6 per cent of GDP.

Index of agricultural production with the triennium ending 1969-70 as base, rose from 71.9 at the end of First Plan to 86.7 at the end of Second Plan. During Third Plan performance of agriculture was not quite satisfactory. Widespread drought during 1965-67 slowed down the rate of growth in agricultural production and led to increased import of foodgrains and other items. Index of agricultural production reached the level of 80.8 in 1965-66 and 80.7 in 1966-67. These drought years also witnessed introduction of the best available agricultural technology for the first time in India in the form of high yield variety programme and multiple cropping programme. The folloeing years recorded substantial improvement in agricultural production. As a result, the index, after recovering to 98.9 points in 1967-68 increased steadily to 112.4 in 1973-74. The next year 1974-75 again a bad year for agriculture when the index declined to 108.6. This was followed by considerable improvement in 1975-76 when it touched 125.1. In 1976-77, the index registered a decline of 8.8 points and stood at 116.3 but again shot up to 132.9 in 1977-78 and 138 in 1978-79. The year 1979-80 witnessed a fall by 21 points when index number of agricultural production slipped to 117. It recovered to 135.3 in 1980-81.

The index number of agriculture production steadily rose to 158.4 in 1985-86. There was decline during 1986-87 to 152.5 and 151.3 in 1987-88. Thereafter it picked up steadily to 192 in 1990-91 and came down to 188.5 in 1991-92 and recovered to 195.8 in 1992-93. According to the revised triennium ending 1981-82 as base, the index numbers of agriculture production which stood at 85.9 in 1970-71 rose to 154.8 in 1993-94. During 1982-83 Kharif production was adversely affected due to wayward monsoon which was inadequate, uneven and untimely. Even so, fall in foodgrains production was only marginal, indicated by a drop of 5.4 points in the production index. Agricultural production registered significant improvement in 1983-84 which was near normal year from the point of view of weather conditions. Index of agricultural production increased from 137.5 in 1982-83 to 156.4 in 1983-84 and production of foodgrains touched a record level of 15,237 crore tonnes. Weather conditions during 1984-85 were not very satisfactory. As a result, production of foodgrains declined to 14,554 crore tonnes and index number of agricultural production also declined marginally to 154.6. During Kharif 1985, onset of the south-west monsoon was delayed over central and northern states and its behaviour during the season was erratic over many states. However, weather conditions during the rabi season were on the whole rather favourable to crop production. Consequently, foodgrains output during 1985-86 stood at 15.044 crore tonnes. Weather conditions during 1986-87 continued to be unsatisfactory. Monsoon was delayed over eastern states, while southern states experienced dry spells leading to moisture stress conditions. As a result only 14.342 crore tonnes of foodgrains production could be achieved during 1986-87. The year 1987-88 witnessed severe drought conditions in most parts of the country and the incidence of heavy floods in the eastern states. The foodgrains production consequently further fell down to 14.035 crore tonnes. During 1988-89 production of foodgrains recorded a new peak of 16,982 crore tonnes indicating a substaintial increase of 1.775 crore tonnes over the previous peak of 15.237 crore tonnes achieved in 1983-84. With the rainfall and weather situation being favourable during south-west monsoon 1989, the total foodgrains production reached another record level of 17.065 crore tonnes.

On account of erratic behaviour of south-west monsoon, foodgrains production in 1991-92 fell by 4.6 per cent to 16.337 crore tonnes from a record level of 17.64 crore tonnes in 1990-91. Production of rice and wheat was 7.467 crore tonnes and 5.676 crore tonnes respectively. There was a substantial decline in the production of coarse cereals and pulses. Production of oilseeds in 1991-92 was less than previous year's production of 18.60 crore tonnes. Production of foodgrains during 1992-93 was 17.948 crore tonnes and the production was recorded at 18.212 crore tonnes in 1993-94. Production of foodgrains during 1994-95 is expected to be of the order of 18.636 crore tonnes.

Production of oilseeds is expected to be around 2.251 crore tonnes. The thrust has been given for the growth and diversification of agriculture to achieve self-sufficiency in food and generate surpluses for exports during the Eighth Five year Plan Period (1992-97).

On the irrigation side the potential created on major, medium and minor schemes increased from 22.6 million ha in 1950-51 to 26.25 million ha at the end of the First Plan, 29.08 million ha by Second Plan, 33.57 million ha at the end of Third Plan 37.1 million ha by 1966-69. At the end of 1969-74 the potential created was 44.10 ha. By 1979-80, it touched 56.61 million ha and by 1984-85, it reached 65.22 million ha. Potential created by 1989-90 was 76.52 million ha by 1991-92, 81.09 million ha and by 1992-93 achievement was 83.01 million ha. The anticipated achievement by 1993-94 is 85.05 million ha. The target for 1994-95 isto create additional irrigation potential of 2.62 million hectare.

Under power sector, total installed capacity (including non-utility), which was only 2301 mw in 1950, increased to 78,367 mw by the end of March 1992. Against the capacity addition of 30,538.7 mw in public utilities envisaged during the Eighth Plan period (1992-97), the actual addition during the first three years (1992-95) were 12,674 mw.

Under the rural electrification programme, 4.70 lakh villages had been electrified out of 5.79 lakh villages (as per 1981 Census) by the end of the Seventh Plan, achieving 81.3 per cent level of electrification. Upto December 1994, 4.94 lakh villages were electrified.

Universal elementary education, eradication of illiteracy in the age group of 15-35 and development of vocational education to act as viable alternate stream have been the focal points of all programmes in the education sector during the Eighth Plan. Major initiatives in the form of Operation Black-board, non-formal education programme, Teacher Education, and District Primary Education Programme have been undertaken to achieve the goal of 'Education for All'. As on September 1993, 108.20 million children have been enrolled in primary schools and 39.91 million in upper primary schools. The Eighth Plan during its first three years could achieve an additional enrolment of 11.69 million in the primary schools and 7.06 million in upper primary sections making a total enrolment of 18.7 million during the Eighth Plan.

The emphasis of adult literacy programme has been on sustainability of literacy skills and the achievement of goals of rmediation, continuation and application of skills of actual living conditions. Total Literacy Campaign (TLC) and Post Literacy and continuing education programmes are designed to cater to the above objectives. The Eighth Plan target was to cover 100 million adult illiterates by 1991. About 41 million people have been made literate so far under various programmes.

Under Vocational Education, the Eighth Plan target is to divert about 11.63 lakh higher secondary students to the vocational stream. Upto the end of 1993-94, 9.12 lakh students were enrolled in 16,450 vocational sections approved in 570 schools. In order to boost the programme and activities in Vocational Education, Pt. Sunder Lal Sharma Central Institute of Vocational Education (PSSCIVE) has been established under NCERT at Bhopal on 1 July 1993.

In the higher education sector as on 1994, there are 153 universities, 34 demand universities, 7,958 colleges and total enrolment in the higher education system is about 48 lakh. In addition, there ia a vast network for technical education, including colleges and institutions offering courses in engineering, medical science, management, etc. In the technical education sector new initiatives like Technology Development Missions, establishemnt off corpus fund in the case of IITs, IIMs and IISc, Banglaore have been taken up recently.

Large investments in the industrial and mineral sector particularly from the beginning of the Second Plan have brought about a significant transformation in the industrial scene. This rate of industrial growth has not been uniform during this period. After a steady growth of about eight per cent during the initial period of 14 years, there was fluctuating trend in the industrial growth rate approaching near stagnancy in 1960-68, going upto a level of 9.6 per cent in 1976-77 and dropping to -1.6 per cent in 1979-80. During the last decade (1970-71 to 1979-80) the average growth rate has been about four per cent per annum. The average growth rate of industry in the Sixth Plan period (1980-85) amounts to nearly six per cent which is a small improvement over the average of about 5.3 per cent in the preceding five years.

Seventh Plan envisaged an average annual growth rate of 8.7 per cent in the output of industry sector. In the first year of the Seventh Plan i.e. 1985-86, the actual growth rate achieved was 8.7 per cent as per revised Index of Industrial Production (IIP) (Base 1980-81=100). In 1986-87, second year of the Seventh Plan, growth rate achieved was 9.2 per cent. However in 1987-88, the growth rate declined to 7.3 per cent due to decline in production towards the end of the year following unprecedented drought. In 1988-89, there was agian a recovery in the growth rate and the IIP recorded an increase to 8.7 per cent. In the last year of the Seventh Plan, there was slight deceleration in the growth rate, which was only 8.6 per cent due to sharp decline in growth rates of mining and electricity sectors. During 1990-91, the growth rate was 8.3 per cent and during

1991-92, the growth rate was 0.6 for industrial production. The industrial production registered an increase of 2.3 per cent in 1992-93 and 4.1 per cent in 1993-94.

Government initiated a number of measures late in Sixth Plan and in early years of Seventh Plan with the objective of removing constraints on industrial growth and providing a more liberal and congenial environment for development of industries. A number of steps were taken to liberalise industrial procedures relating to creation of capacity, imports of technology, etc., to encourage competition in Indian industry so as to ensure reasonable prices and improvement in quality. These include re-endorsement of capacities, delicensing of industries including specified MRTP and FERA industries and broad-banding of a large number of industries especially in areas of high technology industries linked with energy production and utilisation, as well as mass consumer goods industries. Provisions of the MRTP Act and FERA regulations were rationalised to facilitate entry into industrial areas of high priority. Expansion of existing units has been liberalised and investment in moderanisation/renovation/replacement as well as export production, has been exempted from industrial licensing. Licensing of new capacity has been liberalised and concept of minimum economic scale introduced to promote production efficiency, taking advantage of economics of scale.

A number of policy measures have been initiated for development of specific industries like textiles, sugar, steel, electronics, etc. Steps have also been taken to tackle the problem of industrial sickness. These include (i) system for early detection of industrial sickness introduced by Reserve Bank of India' (ii) various steps for checking industrial sickness and promoting industrial revival evolved by Industrial Reconstruction Bank of

India; (iii) setting up of Board for Industrial and Financial rreconstruction, and (iv) setting up of Small Industries Development Fund in IDBI to provide refinancing assistance not only for development, expansion and modernisation but also for rehabilitation of sick industrial units in small scale sector. The statement on industrial policy announced in July 1991 is being implemented. The new industrial policy emphasises delicensing and technological dynamism. Government has also set up modernisation funds for textiles and jute industries to cater to problems of those industries which account for major share of industrial sickness.

The Government is to establish 70 growth centres to act as a nucleus for industrial growth and promote accelerated development especially in backward areas. Sixty nine centres have already been identified. The process of setting up of the growth centres has been started. There has been an important milestone in the public sector steel capactiy with most of the main units of the Stage-I of the Visakhapatnam Steel Plant having come on stream in 1990-91. The 4 MT expansion programmes of Bhillai Steel Plant and Bokaro Steel Plant have also fully materialised during the year.

In order to have more national generalisation, the past performance can be reviewed separately for two categories, i.e., (i) those efforts related to income generation and self-employment and (ii) others related to self-employment-cum-entrepreneurship category.

The first category covers the programmes/schemes under KVIC, TRYSEM, SEEUY and some other institutions exclusively devoted for self-employment. During 1985-86, KVIC, provided employment opportunities to 39.8 lakh persons whose earning amounted to Rs. 349.53 crores. In the total employment under KVIC Programme the share of SC/ST was about

29% and women's participation about 46%. Under TRYSEM Scheme 200,650 youths were to be trained during 1985-86. Out of this, 56,500 youth were trained and 41.845 were reported taking up self-employment.

The second category by and large, refers to SSI entrepreneurs. Under Indian context the two strategies, i.e., developing entrepreneurship and small industries are interwoven. Between 1973-74 and 1986-87, the number SSIs increased by over three folds generation by about two and half times. It is difficult to assess as to how much oif it is the outcome of planned efforts. But programme wise SIDO conducted more than 1638 EDPs and trained 50,130 potential entrepreneurs during 1978-88. During 1970-86 they conducted 287 programme specially for 6,757 engineer entrepreneurs. IDBI sponsored 550 EDPs benefiting 15,369 entrepreneurs. 6 Since its inception NSTEDB sponsored 147 EDPs benefitting 3,090 potential science & technology entrepreneurs. 7 SBI conducted 125 EDPs during 1978-87 and trained 2,939 persons with success rate of 33 percent. NIESBUD masseurs sponsored 42 EDPs benefitting 1125 potential entrepreneurs. Besides such national bodies large number of programmes were conducted locally by other governmental and non-governmental organisations which have not been recorded systematically. As per one estimate about 1,250 full EDPs of 6 weeks duration are conducted every year benefitting more than 40,000 potential entrepreneurs.

Since entrepreneurship development presently pursued by variety of organisations/agencies with different types of approaches/strategies and also with varying degrees of resources for varied target groups, their rate of success (in terms of the ration of number of entrepreneurs who actually set up their enterprises to the number of persons trained/promoted) naturally show a very wide range of variation (8% of 80%). Recently nationwide study by NIESBUD, however, reported 27.8% success rate as national average since there are experiences of higher rates of success there seems to be enough scope for further improvement in all aspects of EDPs starting from Identification & Selection of Potential Entrepreneurs; and Quality & Content of Training; Support Services; and Availability/accessibility to infrastructural facility..

There are very few, if any, published documents presenting quantitative and qualitative evaluation of EDPs. In the absence of uniform data for all reported programmes, it may be useful to consider cost of emploment generation from the typical programmes separately.

The cost of conducting full entrepreneurship development programmes include cost of initial campaign, identification & selection, 4-6 weeks training, and follow-up for about 4-6 months after the completion of training. These can be estimated from the existing pattern of expenditure. SISIs are conducting integrated EDP with an expenditure of Rs. 56,000/- for TCOs and other voluntary organisations who conduct EDPs sponsored by IDBI and other financial institutions; NSTEDB & NIESBUD, the cost comes in between Rs. 70-80 thousand. Under difficult areas and for special schemes such as women entrepreneurship the coast goes upto Rs. 100,000/-. Considerig 30% as success rate and on an average 30 participants per programme the cost for promoting entrepreneurship comes in between Rs. 6000/- and Rs. 11,000/- (without establishment cost) per entrepreneurs who sets up an enterprise with an investment between few thousand to 35 lakhs. SBI Evaluation Study (1986) 10 further help us understand the pattern and size of investment and return by entrepreneurs promoted through such EDPs. The overall average investment by them was reported as Rs. 3.55 lakhs. To be more precise maximum, i.e., 57.4% invested between 2-5 lakhs; and followed by those 27.9% who invested between 1-2 lakhs; and 8% invested upto Rs. 25,000/- and only 6% invested over Rs. 10 lakhs. In terms of benefits, out of such promoted entrepreneurs 83% sampled units reported making on an average a net profit of Rs. 48,200/- (about 4000/- per month) during 1985.

Another study that provided detailed information about cost/benefit refers to Assam Experiment-Self-Employment through entrepreneurship Motivation Training Centres during 1973-76. With the total expenditure of Rs. 17.96 lack that included the cost of training of officers, all recurring and non-recurring expenditrue of 6 EMTCs in Assam 534 units started functioning (another 593 received financial sanction but not considered for calculating benefits here) and accordingly the cost for promoting each succeessful entrepreneur was reported having net profit between Rs. 300/- to Rs. 1500/- per month (during mid seventies). Further the total amount raised and invested by these entrepreneurs in the area amount raised and invested by these entrepreneurs in the area amounted to Rs. 1.2 crores to which Govt. contributed only 12.26 lakhs as seed money. The evauation study further revealed that more than 90% units thus established provided employment to 1-2 persons besides the self-employed owner.

Another valuable and more recent information related to cost-benefit of a typical entrepreneurship development programme for self-employment (in SBI sector) is available with Rural Development Self-emploment Training Institute (RUDSETI), Gurgaon which has been set up jointly by a Trust and two nationalised banks since 1984. RUDSETI trained 1,832 candidates and

1127 of them have already set up their enterprises, the total of cost on selection, two weeks training counselling and support activities comes to Rs. 795/- per successful self-employed entrepreneurs (this does not include the establishment cost). In addition, the bank financing to these entrepreneurs on an average was reported as Rs. 18,214/- per self-employed person, enterprises set up by these entrepreneurs represented 'business' enterprises 28.7% followed by 'industries' 19.6% and 11.6% 'service units'. It was further revealed that 68% of thus promoted entrepreneurs have started earning net profit between Rs. 500/- to Rs. 1500/- per month.

A number of new measures have been suggested to improve the operational efficiency of planned programmes. Some of these can be cited below:

Planning by its very nature is a participative process in which both the Union government and State governments will collaborate with each other both in formulation and implementation of plans. It has also been suggested in the approach paper to provide additional funds to the poorer States si as to improve their basic minimum services and inter-State allocations would be determined on the basis of identified gaps which deprive people of the benefit of development.

Another irritant of development inbthe planning process is the Centrally-sponsored schemes (CSS). In 1996-96, there were 182 CSS with a total outlay of Rs. 16,000 crore. Many of these schemes relate to subjects falling squarely within the competence of the State governments. It is now proposed that inter-State schemes will remain under the control of the Central government. All other schemes where state management will have operational efficiency would be transferred to the States along with caresponding funds. This will go a long way in improving the operational efficiency of such schemes and establishng better relationship between the Centre and the States. Approximately, half of the total planned public investment is expected to go into agricultural and rural development.

The process of decentralization and grant of autonomy does not stop at the state level, it has to be carried further to the Panchayats. Democratic decentralization through Panchayati raj though established in the fifties in some of the States, did not make any impact in the process of planning. The 73rd constitutional amendment has now changed the contours of decentralized planning. The State governments are now required to endow the Panchayats with the power and authority necessary to enable them to function as institutions of self-government with the responsibility of preparing plans for economic developmint and social justice and implementing them. In the IX Plan, 29 subjects identified in the Eleventh Schedule would be transferred to the Panchayati Raj institutions along with resources and personnel engaged in such works. This will usher in a new era of people-oriented planning in which not only the governments at the Centre and the States, but the people at large, particularly the poor, can fully participate. Participatory planning is essential both for accelerated growth and ensuring social justice.

As we have already said, the growth of population may create tremandous difficulty in increasing employment or improving the economic well-being of the poor. The current high growth of population is mainly due to (a) the large size of the population in the reproductive age-group (estimated contribution 60%), (b) higher fertility due to unmet need for contraception (estimated contribution 20%), and (c) high wanted fertility due to the prevailing high IMR (estimated contribution about 20%). In the IX Plan, special efforts are proposed to be taken to meet all the feltneeds of contraception and reduce the infant and maternal morbidity and mortallity so that there is a reduction in the desired level of fertility. Attempts would be made also to enhance the quality and coverage of family welfare programme by involving medical practioners of all types; Panchayati Raj institutions, industry, agriculture and labour representatives. Along with this, greater emphasis would be given on education and health programmes which would go a long ways in reduting the rate of growth of population.

There has been a considerable sloppage in the growth of capacity in the infrastructure sector during the VIII Plan. Several measures are suggested to improve the efficiency and capacity utilization of the exiting infrastructural assets. First, greater emphasis will be given to complete ongoing projects so that they start yielding returns as early as possible. Secondly, since this in itself may not meet the requirements of the demand, additional facilities would be ensured for increase in the resource availability for further investment and proper maintenance of existing infrastructural facilities. There is a tendency now to get too many projects cleared without the requisite financial resources in sight which not only causes delay in completion of projects but unnecessarily escalates costs many more times than the original estimate. Project planning would be screened and only those projects would be sanctioned for which funds are in sight and which could be completed early without cost overruns.

In addition, a number of other specific measures are proposed to improve the economic well-being and quality of life. The empowerment of social groups like SCs, STs, OBCs, women and minorities is of crucial importance. A high priority is accorded to empowering these soecial groups both economically and socially to enable them to join the mainstream of national development at the earlist.

Environmental degradation has creaated great damage to the economy. It has also adversely affected the gealth of people. There is a proposal to ensure environmental sustainability of the development process through social mobilization and participation of people at all levels.

In spite of increased production of agricultural commodities, a large number of people are still on the verge of destitution. It is, therefore, proposed to ensure food and nutritional security for all, particualarly the vulnerable sections of the community.

There is a great deal of regional imbalance operating at both inter-State and the intra-State levels. with greater freedom and choice of location that is now available to industry, it is more than likely that some States and some regions would be able to attract more private investment than others. In such a case, more public resourcces should be invested invested in such backward regions.

Self-reliance has been one of the main features of planning in India. In spite of the poening of the economy to international agencies, self-reliance would remain n important component of development policy and strategy. The Ninth Plan would address the issues of external vulnerability and develop suitable strategies for making India a strong and confident player in the international economy.

Planning for sustainable regional development

Ecologically sustainable economic development has become a policy issue of major significance. conceptualizing and analysing sustainable development is very important at the regional level. This paper investigates sustainable in a practical planning context and seeks to highlight the notions of sustainable resource use. Economics provides some guidelines for planning responsibilities, although ecological considerations should also be taken into account. A region is a geographical area consisting of a coherent entity from the standpoint of description, analysis, administration, planning, or policy. Among the various types of regions are homogenous and functional regions. Functional environmental regions are often based on the interactions between environmental resources like ground-water, river, and meteorological systems within a particular region. Homogenous environmental regions are based on the existence of common resources in the area concerned. Regions can also be distinguished as natural regions, economic regions, administrative regions, etc.

Regional development is often critically dependent on the regional availability of resources. A region's economic development may be directly dependent on the resources in the region. Usually, in such cases the dependence is on resources that may serve as essential and cheap productive inputs for economic activities. Concomitantly, the environmental capacity to absorb waste materials and pollution can restrict economic activity. Some regions may depend on export of resources as the main source of income. A regional resource sector may have several effects on the activities in a region such as increased demand for public services, utilities, and infrastructure; demand for labour; capital, space and spin-offs to other private sectors. Thus, the development of a resource sector might lead to shifts in sector allocation, income levels, distribution, and exchange rates.

From the standpoint of welfare, regional sustainable development ensures that the regional population attains an acceptable level of welfare both at present and in the future and that this regional development is not only compatible with ecological circumstances in the long run but also tries to accomplish a globally sustainable development. Consequently, regional sustainable development has to fulfil the following goals:

— It should ensure the regional population a sustained acceptable level of welfare;

— It should not have conflict with sustainable development at a supraregional level;

— It should ensure economic progress and/or developoment of potential of the region concerned;

— It should maintain ecological values and/or relieve constraints of the area concerned; and

— It should ensure the economic and environmental interest of the parties involved.

The economic-ecological interactions arise in general, because concerted socio-economic development requires a compromise between material growth and environmental parameters, including environmental quality and vital natural resources. Although in the short run, the conflict between material growth and environmental quality may be severe, in the long run, a mitigating effect may emerge, because continued economic growth needs a sound resource base and structural protection and upgrading of environmental quality.

Such a coevolutionary development, in both the developed and the developing countries takes for granted that the economy and the ecology ultimately do not conflict with each other. Such coevolution is also based on equitable development options for the present and future generations. It does not necessarily require mutual positive spill-over effects between the economy and the ecology. This idea is echoed in the notion of ecologically sustainable economic development.

This paper, investigates sustainable development in a practical planning context and seeks to highlight the notion of sustainable resource use. An attempt has also been made to provide a practical framework, as renewable stocks of natural resources are key factors of sustainable development.

Indeed at the local level, resources like land, labour and human and physical resources—physical capital to a limited extent are available. Techno—economic surveys can identify the potential resources. But will all the labour force be mobilized for gainful and productive employment? This is a more important task and accompllishing ths depends on the integration of the techno—economic approach with other aspect of the social system and development process. This is the concern of many mono—disciplines like economics, engineering, sociology, psychology, etc. All such studies have pointed out that only at the local level, the basic needs, particularly of vulnerable sections can be identified and they justify larger investment in primary education for promoting health, nutrition, rural development, family size, fertility, literacy and awareness of national culture.

It is true that rural development is in the main equivalent to the development of food and cash croops and their needed inputs—irrigation, fertilizer, seeds and other resource inputs—animal husbandry, dairying and poultry farming, fisheries, forestry and agro—industries. (Dr. Malcolm S. Adisheshiah in Bulletin of Madras Institute of Development Studies, January 1991 P.41). But such investments in agricultural developmentare bound to be more effective when there is adequate investment in human resource development, particularly in literacy and primary education. Between the I and VII Five Year Plans, there has been a decline in agriculture, forestry, animal husbandry, fisheries irrigation, rural development and village and cottage industry from Rs. 45,924.70 crore to Rs. 45,523.02 crore (ie from 54.92% to 23.62% of the total public sector outlay). But in spite of the decline in agricultural outaly, rural development culd have been quickened if only there had been more investment in human resources and human developmen. Local resource mobilization with local planning seems to be a promising vehicle for promoting rural development and alleviating poverty.

Local resource mobilization and substitution of human capital as well as physical capital is in conformity with the experience of some of the Scandinaviancountriesand Japan in this context. Theyhave been able to substitute the scarce resources with resource mobilizaton at the local level in rural and agricultural sectorsin particular. Such local resources cannot flow to higher levels but can improve productivity at the local level. This resource augmenting effect has the advatage of accelerating agricultural growth.

In such an effort, equity will have to be given special consideration. The disadvantaged population has to be seen not in therole ofobjects of participation but they are to be integrated as the subjects ofoperation. There should be also anb organizational structure which promotes the effective participation of the disadvantagedpopulation. The emergence of local bodies with elected representatives, one hopes, will make it possible to privide thisinfrastructure.

There should be sound planning at the three levels of District Panchayats, Panchayat Samithis and Village Panchayats.

Underutilization may be in the intensity of land use and agricultural productivity or the levels of utilisation of labour force. Measures ofunderutilization can be: (a) a straightforward measure of idle resources, of production capacity at a given level of technology and organization, eg fallow land, unemployment and underemployment according to atime measure; (b) misallocation of resources due to lack of knowledge of superior alternatives or distortion in the structure okf incentives; and (c) underutilization in terms of productivity. According to Prof. Brahmananda, even though aggregate capital may be adequate potentially at the macrolevel, capital in the form of wage goods capacity may be deficient. It is in the process of production of wage goods at the local level through local planning that local resource mobilization can take place and productivity can be improved and social change brought about. At the grass roots level in the rural areas, there is urgent need for improving productivity and promoting social change with better education.

Rural development refers to a number of development programmes. Earlier it was linked only with agricultural development but on the basis of the experience during the last few decades we can speak of holistic rural development which includes agriculture, rural development, rural indutries, and hollistic self—supporting development.

In order to accelerate such a holistic rural development there are three major potential areas for integration which are: (a) stepping up the existing wage employment programme in rural areas ofor capital construction in agriculture and for ecodevelomen; (b) stimulating the growth of households by intergrating them with the existing self—employment programmes like IRDP; and (c) accelerating the pace of social development.

In sum, we will emphasize that poverty alleviation programmes should be properly integratd with over—all development. No rural development is possible without wipping out p[overty or reducing it in stages. The integration of poverty alleviation objective with the over–all development strategy has to be distinguished from the issue of integrating poverty alleviation programmes with the over–all development strategy. The over—all development strategy is concerned with questions like investment priorities, choice of technique and location of projects through trickle down effects. It tries to reduce poverty. A greater and more specific role has to be given to investment in agiven resources, eg bringing down the capital output ratio to a certain level sector by sector). But integration of poverty alleviation programmes with over–all development strategy tries to ensure that poverty alleviation programmes subserve the goals of over—all development. At present, the schemes for increasing incomes and employment do not adequately take care of it. In this also there should be a greater role both for human resource development and human development.

Sustainable regional planning

Sustainable development has become a key catch-phrase in eonomic planning and resource management. However, the interpretation of this concept is still obscure, and definitions of it are abundant ranging from continued economic growth to steady economics where economic growth to steady state economies where economic growth mainly serves to compensate for environmental degradation.

Sustainability, as defined by the Brundtland Commission, is essentially a holistic notion, and as such all aspects of the system need to be included in it. Now, the same may also be defined as the preservation of the production possibilities of an economy to produce useful goods and services. Such a definition could provide some guidance on the rate at which one can exploit exhaustible resources or the level of degradation of renewable resources that may be permitted. However, this raises another issue that in the production of such goods and services, man-made capital and natural resources (we can call the latter environmental capital) can substitute for each other, at least within some limits.

In this context, it is essential to evolve techniques for planning and decision-making with a view to working out a viable programme for sustainable development. The tools of benefit-costs analysis and project appraisal need to be so recast as to combine the traditional economic efficiency criterion with the criterion of sustainable development. The problem of discounting the future streams of benefits and costs and the choice of appropriate discount rate assume especial significance in this regard. The concept of benefits and costs will have to be redefined to take account of the effect of a project on environment and sustainability of development in the long-run.

Gives the levels of development of States on the basis of the following determinants: (1) Per capita net State domestic product, (2) Unemployment rate, (3) Poverty ratio, (4) Per capita education expenditure, (5) Literacy rate, (6) Infant mortality rate, (7) Annual population growth rate, etc.

Adjudged on the basis of the statistical evidence, the five most backward States in India in terms of socio-economic development are Uttar Pradesh, Orissa, Bihar, Madhya Pradesh and Rajasthan. These States are extremely backward not only in terms of economic development but also by the levels of their per capita net State domestic product. It can also be said that states with higher per capita income tend to do well in terms of overall socio-economic development as well. Kerala, however, is an exception to this rule and proves that a high success rate in social development is possible with higher levels of expenditure in the social sectors even when the levels of per capita income in a State is low.

The region's natural resources used as goods are ground-water for drinking and irrigation and timber for paper and pulp. The ecosystems provide services of outdoor recreation and nature conservation while they assimilate surplus ammonium and nitrate from nature. Land is the most important resource in the region and any model that deals with the problems of land use and changes in the quality of land is of considerable interest. Land pressure in various districts of the region is fairly high, particularly in small districts, given the available technology and the production constraints in such semi-arid parts of the region. Land pressure is particularly important in case of overstocking.

The critical success factors in coping with the problems of land pressure are the following:

— Controlling population growth in the areas concerned;

— Ensuring balanced livestock development;

— Controlling land alienation, mainly in smaller districts; and

— Controlling technological developments and related policies regarding boreholes.

Ecologically sustainable economic development has become a policy issue of major significance. Conceptualizing and analyzing sustainable development is clearly important at the regional level. The openness of a spatial system evokes the question of environmental sacrifices in space and time. When the issue of the substitutability of environmental decay is at stake, the related concept of weak and strong sustainability requires further exploration on the basis of a thorough investigation of underlying welfare concepts and associated collective welfare function.

In order to obtain a homostatic balance of resources in space and time, much attention has to be given to regional resource accounting. Efficiency, equity and externality aspects of resource use can then be given due emphasis, while attempts at valuing unpriced resources may provide a sound basis for project appraisal. Geographic information systems may be helpful to visualize all relevant policy aspects. In many cases, governments in an attempt to cope with environmental deterioration, have misjudged the causes of such decay and have even aggravated the original conditions. Thus, a closer analysis of the costs and remedies regarding both signal and response failures would be desirable. In the context of sustainable regional development, critical sucess factors refer to major focal points for policy intervention. Identification of such factors may induce proactive sustainability of policies. In sustainable regional development planning, where regions are open, critical success factors may also be found outside the specific region.

7

Future Prospects

As per the quick estimates of the Index of Industrial Production, the overall growth of industrial production during April-June 1996 was 8.5 per cent over the corresponding period of 1995 with the following sectoral contributions.

As per the use based classificaton of industries, the overall growth has been broad based. After being relatively sluggish in the last two years, Intermediate Goods have recorded a growth of 11.9% in April-June 1996.

Industrial performance based on the production of 172 industries which together have a weight of 88% of IIP indicate a growth of 9.98 per cent in April-June, 1996. There has been deceleration in the growth of certain core sectors such as electricity, crude petroleum, steel, fertilizers, ferro alloys, jute manufacturers etc.

The first five months of the current financial year witnessed a sharp drop in the growth rate of infrastructure industries to 3.5% from 7.8% for the corresponding period of 1995-96. Amongst the industries that declined are: crude petroleum at (-)10.4% from 7.2%, electricity at 2.4% from 8.2% and saleable steel at 4.6% from 8.5%.

The performance of six Infrastructure Industries which is a critical indicator of the overall health.

The Office of Economic Adviser (OEA) also collects

advance information on the production of 24 selected industries which have a weight of around 50% in the IIP. According to the information available, these industries have recorded a growth of 5.8% during April-July, 1996.

As per the information provided by CMIE, the corporate sector recorded a robust 22% growth in sales during 1995-96. This was particularly impressive because it comes after an unsually high increase of 23% recorded during 1994-95. The growth was reasonably well spread over major industry groups. In particular, the automobiles group, the chemicals sector and machinery industry performed exceptionally well.

About a quarter of the companies surveyed recorded sales growth rates less than 10%. At the same time, a little over a quarter of the companies recorded growth rates of more than 50%. Growth was mostly concentrated amongst companies with a size of Rs.75 crore to Rs.100 crore in terms of sales.

Interest payment by the corporate sector increased at a faster pace (nearly 24%) compared to the growth in sales. High interest cost during the year adversely affected most companies except the very large ones. However, the higher interest cost did not dampened sales growth in 1995-96.

According to the report of the RPG Foundation, the performance of non-finance companies was the highest during 1995-96 when compared to the other years in the 90s. Despite the liquidity crunch, the companies fared well mainly due to high and relatively inelastic demand for industrial goods, increased velocity of circulation of money, better inventory management and a decline in the incremental capital output ratio of the corporate sector. Thus despite paying a higher interest of at least 3% points more, there was a marginal improvemeant in the average rate of capital employed and the net profitability of the corporate sector.

Advance indications of the corporate performance for the first half of 1996-97 are now becoming available. These indicate a slow down in sales growth to around 9 per cent compared to over 24 per cent in the previous year. With inflation at around 5 per cent, real sales growth is around 4-5 per cent. Inventory levels are also increasing and with that interest burden. The liquidity crunch witnessed in 1995-96 and resultant high interest rates are affecting corporate investment in the current year.

In a period of weak sales growth, one normally excepts a high inventory holdings. However, continued high interest rates in last few years has resulted in better inventory management and the inventory levels have been declining continuously. These were around 20 per cent of sales in 1995-96. Even a significant increase in inventory holdings will not make much difference to the production levels.

NCAER regularly conducts a Survey of Industrial Confidence. According to the latest information available the business confidence index for August has sharply declined indicating that second half of 1996-97 may be even worse than the first half. Psychologically the corporate sector is now excepting a slow down in industrial activity and the inertia of this deceleration may result in a slow down greater than what economic fundamental may indicate.

In a wide spectrum of industry and agriculture and the entire gamut of services, there has been great progress in the country during the post-Independence era. The growth in several sectors have indeed been spectacular and in several others it has been modest while in a few others outright dismal. On Monday, 10 November 1996, the foundation stone for the automobile plant of the Hyundai Motor Company of South Korea, was laid at Irungattukottai, some 40 km from Chennai. The plant involves an outlay of $ 700 million (around Rs. 2500 crore) in the first phase; and another $ 400 million (around Rs. 1440 crore) in the second phase. A production capacity of around 100,000 passenger cars in the 1300 cc-1500 cc range is envisaged.

The first car is expected to roll out of the assembly line by October 1998. Most importantly, HMC promises a 70 per cent indigenous content from the first car. Which means prospects for dozens of additonal collaboration arrangements and investments for the production of components. At full production, the turnover of HMC will be in the region of Rs. 6000 crore.

This is the third mega investment in the automobile sector involving outlays exceeding Rs. 1500 crore each. The other two relate to the Mahinndra-Ford India Ltd. project to produce passenger cars of similar capacity and in same medium segment; and by Ashok Leyland Ltd., planning to invest on facilities to expand capacity to 100,000 commercial vehicles.

In recent months total investments promised in Tamil Nadu exceed Rs. 5000 crore–an outlay that perhaps exceed all investments made on new projects in the first instance all through the past 50 years.

In all these areas, and in a wide spectrum of industry and agriculture and the entire gamut of services, there has been great progress through the years of Independent India. The growth in several sectors have indeed been spectacular and in several others, it had been modest; and in a few others outright dismal. The bench-making has been done both in regard to the potential offered by India and by developments in several other countries which started on industrialisation much later than we did. South Korea offers a ready example.

In looking at growth, over the last five decades, we can segment these into five distinct phase that roughly correspond with decennial slots.

In accordance with the prevailing thinking, the First Five year Plan stated that the objective of industrial planning was to make good the deficiencies in production of key industrial items and to initiated development, which would enable cumulative expansion of such basic production. There was better appreciation in the First Plan of the need for coordination of industrial planning with the formulation of other economic policies, such as customs and excise tariff structure, import and export policy, investment and technology policy and monetary and financial policy. The Second Plan and later plans have been encreasingly concerned with the allocation of public resources and much less with indications oand policies to direct the whole economy indesired directions.

The Industrial Policy Statement of 1973, inter alia, identified high-priority industries where investment from large industrial houses and foreign companies would be permitted. The Industrial Policy Statement of 1980 focussed attention on the need for promoting competition in domestice market, technological upgradation and modernisation. The policy laid the foundation for an increasingly competitive export base and for encouraging foreign investment in high priority technology areas. This found expression in the Sixth Five Year Plan, which emphasised the need for productivity to be the central concern in all economic and production activities.

Nevertheless the sector continued to provide the thrust for the development of heavy industries. In critical areas such as power, railways, coal, petroleum, steel and fertilisers, the public sector has been intensely involved in setting the pace of development. Apart from public investments in basic industry and infrastructure, the expansion of the private sector in line with Plan objectives and priorities were greatly facilitated by financial institutions. An elaborate network of specialised development banking institutions with the Industrial Development Bank of India at the apex was established to help finance industrial investment in the private sector. These institutions, numbering over 50, have become the major source of long-term finance for the corporate sector.

Development in sixth and seventh plans

As the statement on Industrial Policy, 1991 says, "These policies created a climate for rapid industrial growth in the country. Thus on the eve of the Seventh Five year Plan, a broad-based infractructure had been built up. Basic industries had been established. A high degree of self-reliance in a large number of items–raw materials, intermediates, finished goods—had been achieved. New growth centres of industrial activity had emerged, as had a new generation of entrepreneurs. A large number of engineers, technicians and skilled workers has been trained."

The Sixth Plan had achieved augmentation of new capacity more or less in consonance with the targets in alarge number of insdustries including, among others, aluminium, zinc, lead thermoplastics, yarn, petrochemical intermediates, electrical equipment, cement and consumer durables. However shortfall in production had taken place in some basic industries, such as steel, cement, non-ferrous metals, fertilisers and certain other industries, including textiles, jute manufactures, sugar, drugs and pharmaceuticals, commercial vehicles and railway wagons. Production targets were exceed in a few industries like machine toos, passenger cars, motor cycles and scooters, consumer electronics and communication equipment. Domestic imbalances resulting from shortfalls in production hasd to be corrected through imports of essential commodities, like steel, cement, fertilisers and sugar.

A technological thrust was given during the Plan period in certain industries in the engineering sector. The first 500 MW thermal generating unit was commissioned and the manufacture of 500 MW turbo generators and boilers had commenced. There has been a systematic upgradation of production technology for other equipment, needed by the power sector. The manufacture of equipment for 1350 tonnes per day fertiliser units and blast furnaces of 3200 cubic metres capacity for steel plants was being undertaken in the country. A strong base had been laid for the rapid development of the electronics sector.

The Seventh Plan recognised the need to consolidate on these strengths and to take initiatives to prepare Indian industry to respond effectively to the emerging challenges. A number of policy and procedural changes which were introduced in 1985-86 aimed at increasing productivity, reducing costs and improving quality. Production capacity restrictions on the industries were gradually reduced and broad banding, which enabled a manufacturer to choose and produce any product mix which suited him in the context of the prevailing market conditions was introduced.

In 1986, as against a policy of re-endorsement of existing capacity, the scheme of minimum economic scale of production was introduced with Letters of Intent prescribing a minimum economic size for a single unit. The accent was on opening the domestic market to increased competition and readying the industry to stand on its own in the face of international competition. The public sector was freed from a number of constraints and given a large measure of autonomy. The technological and managerial modernisation of industry was pursued as the key instrument for increasing productivity and improving competitiveness in the world.

As a result of the policies pursued since Independence, the long term trend of industrial growth for over forty years since 1950 is a trend annual growth of just over 6 per cent. This, says rakesh MOhan in an essay in Bimal Jalan's book on Indian Economy, "is quite an achievement, given the magnitude of distortions built into the system." He divides the growth record into three distinct periods: 7.7 per cent annual growth over the first three plan periods (1950-1965), four per cent annual growth over the holiday (1966-69) and the Fourth and Fifth Plan periods (1969-79), and finally the recovery to about 7.7 per cent growth over the Sixth and Seventh periods.

The period 1966-1980, says Mohan is effectively the dark period for Indian economy. This period encompassed a number of exogenous shocks: the devastating three-year drought of 1965-68, the aftermath of increased defence espenditures resulting from 1962 was with China and two wars with Pakistan, the oil price shocks of 1973 and 1979, and the downturn in the availability of foreign resources. During this period, the Indian economy was constantly struggling to adjust.

As a result of policy changes, the composition of Indian industry had undergone great transformation. At Independence, the consumer goods industry accounted for almost half of all industrial production. In 1991 such industries accounted for only about 20 per cent. In contrast, capital goods production was less than 4 per cent of total industrial production. In 1991, it had gone up to 24 per cent. Similarly basic goods share had increased from 20 per cent to 40 per cent.

Attainment of industrialisation over the last 48 years has been striking feature of Indian economic development process which was launched as a conscious and deliberate policy in the early fifties. In pursuance of this policy, large investment has been made in building up capacity over a wide spectrum of industries. Industrial production has made rapid strides in terms of variety, quality and quantity. There has been a substantial diversification of industrial base during this period with the consequent ability to produce a very broad range of industrial goods. Self-reliance has been achieved in basic and capital good. Indigenous capabilities have now been established to the point of virtual self-sufficiency so that further expansion in various sectors such as mining, irrigation, power chemicals, transport and communication can be based primarily on indigenous equipment. Process of industrialisation has also fostered entrepreneurship and development of a wide variety of technical, managerial and operative skills. Today, the country is in a position to provide consultancy services as well as managers, technicians and skilled workers for setting up industrial projects aborad.

The Industrial Policy Resolution of 1948 marked the beginning of the evolution of Indian Industrial Policy. The resolution not only defined the broad contours of the policy, it delineated the role of the State in the industrial development both as an entrepreneur and as an authority.

Successive policy resolutions also reiterated this

basic tilt in favour of the public sector. The Industrial Policy Resolution of 1956 gave the public sector a strategic role in the economy. It categorised industries which would be the exclusive responsibility of state or would progressively come under state control and others. Earmarking the pre-eminent position to the public sector, it envisaged private sector co-existing with the State and thus attempted to give the policy framework flexibility.

The Industrial Policy initiatives undertaken by Government since July 1991 have been designed to build on the past industrial achievements and to accelerate the process of making Indian industry internatinally competitive. It recognises the strength and maturity of the industry and attempts to provide the competitive stimulus for higher growth. The thrust of these initiatives has been to increase domestic and external competition through extensive application of market mechanism and facilitating forging of dynamic relationships with foreign investors and suppliers of technology. The process of reform has been continuous.

As on 31 March 1993 there were 245 central public sector undertakings, comprising of eight in the construction sector, 72 in services and remaining 165 in the manufacturing. The number of CPSUs as indicated above exclude nine companies, six insurance companies and three financial institutions with Central Government investment but without direct responsibility of management.

The total capital employed in the 245 CPSUs increased from Rs. 1,179.91 billion in 1991-92 to Rs. 1,399.33 billion in 1992-93. The overall rate of return on capital employed in the PSUs also increased from 2.0 per cent in 1991-92 to 2.43 per cent in 1992-93.

The number of small scale units as at the end of 31

March 1994 were 2.38 million comprising of 1.77 million registered units and 0.61 un-registered. The overall production in the small scale sector during 1993-94 has been estimated to have reached Rs. 2,416.5 billion. The total value of exports of these units has been Rs. 177.85 billion in 1992-93.

India has made rapid strides in industrialization, and today is one of the ten most industrialized nations of the world. But industrialization, as in the rest of the world, has brought with it unwanted and unanticipated consequences. These include unplanned urbanization, pollution and risk of accidents. Industrialization moreover not only affects the immediate environment, but has consequences for a larger region whose resources get intimately tied to new industrial development.

Yet as the country continues to industrialize and new plants come up, some of the underlying issues remain. Dirty industries continue moving South. Hazardous chemicals are dumped or brought for reprocessing to developing countries. Often, in developed countries, different values are attached to human life in the North and in the South. Different standards are applied, and processes and factories being discarded in developed countries get relocated in the developing ones.

The Bhopal disaster, when methyl isocyanate crept into the houses of sleeping residents on the morning of 3 December, 1984, killing over 3,000 people and maiming countless others for life, brought many of these issues into sharp focus. It was a tragic testimony of just how much could go wrong. The hazardous side of industry became painfully apparent to countless people in India and abroad. It questioned location policies, safety requirements of industries, the responsibilities of North-based multinational corporations, the preparedness for dealing with disasters, citizens' right to know about the industrial process and the risks involved.

Near the industries, water and air pollution problems are very serious. Water pollution not only affects surface water but also groundwater. It is estimated that 70 per cent of India's surface water is seriously polluted and 80 per cent of the population does not have access to safe drinking water. For instance in Patancheru in Andhra Pradesh, over 60 factories—most of them chemical units—discharge their toxic wastes into freshwater streams. In Bichhri in Rajasthan, chemical effluents from textile and chemical industries pollute the waters of rivers and wells. The health impact of such cases is serious and the incidence of cancer, lung and skin diseases, and deformities is high in these areas. While they are restricted in extent, air pollution levels are high in industrial areas. For instance the average levels of particulate matter in the four metropolitan cities exceeds 360 mg/m while the WHO standard is 150 mg/m.

Another concern relates to occupational health incertain industries. Asbestosis, byssinosis and pneumonoconiosis are some of the occupational diseases reported. Silicosis has been reported in mines and other industries.

Several central and state statues, such as the Industrial Development Act, the Labour Acts, the Factories Act and the Municipal Acts have environmental provisions in them. However it was the enactment of the Water (Prevention and Control of Pollution) Act, 1974, and the Air (Prevention and Control of Pollution) Act, 1981, which made these environmental factors the principal object of legislation. The Bhopal tragedy caused a surge in environmental legislation and an umbrella Environment (Protection) Act was passed in 1986. This covers hazardous activities in addition to pollution.

Under the Environment (Protection) Act, 1986, the Central Government is responsible for laying down procedures and safeguards for handling hazardous substances. Rules have been made for the manufactures, storage and import of hazardous chemicals, their management and handling, as well as for the manufacture, use, import and storage of micro-organisms and genetically engineered organisms. Radioactive waste disposal is controlled through a regulatory board managed by the Bhabha Atomic Research Centre. The Government has also established a Central Crises Group Alert System with a control room at New Delhi to deal with major chemical accidents in the country.

Many industries and large projects need environmental clearance. The State Pollution Control Boards monitor industrial areas. The Government of India has made it mandatory to assess the environmental impact of new large undertaking in the country. The impact assessment covers not only air, water and soil polluiton, but also damage to historical monuments, wildlife, forests, and to natural resources in general. Unique to India is the recently enacted Mandatory Public Liability Insurance which makes it imperative for units dealing with hazardous substances to take insurance cover against damage to health or property of the community in the vicinity of the industry.

Industrial location policy is a crucial element in determining the impact of industry on the environment. Unplanned industrial growth has in some cases led to industrail conglomerates and urban sprawl. This has often led to prime agricultural and forest land being diverted for urban and industrial use. Near forests, urban areas have led to deforestation. For certain industries, a two-stage clearance procedure has been adopted by the Ministry of Environment and Forests, considering the site specific nature.

While legislation today has enabled authorities to step in, this alone cannot lead to improved environment in and around industries. For this to happen public awareness, as well as awareness and concern among the decision-makers is required. Where people have been consicous they have protested and not let polluting industries spoil their environment. Where industries have been conscious they have got together and taken initiatives for effluent treatment. A typical example of joint efforts by industry in the safe disposal of effluents is the Baroda Effluent Channel in Gujarat, managed by the Gujarat Industrial Development Corporation.

There is urgent need to create widespread awareness. Towards this end the Ministry of Environment and Forests has made a beginning by introducing a scheme for an Ecomark to lable environment-friendly products. NGOs too have several programmes to create environmental consciouness. School programmes to involve students in environmental quality monitoring have begun.

But finally environmental factors will only be taken into account where alternatives are availabel. Today with Indai opening up its economy to greater internationl participation in the industrialization of the country, it si important to ensure that the best and cleansest technologies are available for htis growth, so that industrialization occurs with the minimum of negative consequences.

As a result of sound policies pursued over the years, tremendous development has taken place in India industry, which stands today on a sound footing. However, there are certain infrastructural weaknesses which need to be tackled to ensure further growth. Indian industry has undergone a sea change since Independence. From a situation, where even a pin had to be inported, India has reached a stage when it is going to manufacture 50-seater and 100-seater passenger aircraft. What is more, the Indian consumer today has a wide variety of goods to choose from. The Indian market place is today loaded with a range of goods. Whether it is newer models of cars, scooters or mlobikes, washing machines, sooking range or mixies there ia large variety to choose from. Gone are the days when choices were limited and one had to wait almost a year to get delivery of a new car or a scooter. One can today walk into a show room and drive out. With a choice available to the consumer the quality of goods have also shown distinct improvement.

Indian industry at the time of Independence was at a rudimentary stage. It was confined to cotton and jute textiles, which accounted for 56.8 per cent of value-added in manufacturing sugar (6.6 per cent), engineering (8.4 per cent), steel (7.6 per cent), chemicals (4.1 per cent) and cement (2.1 per cent). Modern industry formed only six to eight per cent of national income in Independence India in 1950, with small scale enterprises and mining contributing 12 to 14 per cent. A feature of India's industrial sector soon after Independence was the virtual absence of capital or producers goods industry. Indian industries had to rely almost wholly on imported machinery and machine tools. In 1950, India met 89.8 per cent of its need for machine tools through imports, producing internally only Rs. 30 lakh worth of machine tools and portable tools.

The foundations of modern India's industrial economy was laid by Jawaharlal Nehru, who led the country to freedom and thereafter as Prime Minister for nearly 17 years, built the country's economy form a scratch. This was done through the public sector, whose foundations were laid by Nehru, as the private sector did not have the resources to undertake huge infrastructure projects, like Bhakra hydro-electric power project, or steel plants like Bhilai, whom the great visionary described as the temples of modern India. Nehru realised that without the basic infrastructure industries, the foundations of a modern industrial economy could not be laid. If this war true in 1950, it is equally true today as infrastructural bottlenecks are constraining growth.

Policy resolutions

Industrial growth after Independence was facilitated by the Industrial Policy Resolution of 1948, followed by the Industrial Policy Resolution of 1956, which had as its objective, the acceleration of the rate of economic growth and the speeding up of industrialisation as a means of achieving a socialist pattern of Society. In 1956 capital was scarce and the base of entrepreneurship was not strong enough. Hence the 1956 Industrial Policy Resolution, gave primacy to the role of the state to assume predominant and direct responsibility for industrial development. Special importance was given in the two resolutions of 1948 and 1956 to the development of steel, heavy engineering, machine tools and heavy chemicals industry.

The industrial policy resolution of 1948 has a small number of industries to be reserved for production by the public sector. These included the production and control of atomic energy and ownership and managment of railways. However, coal, iron and steel, aircraft manufacturing, shipbuilding, manufacture of telegraph and wireless equipment (except radios) and minerals were reserved for production by Central or State government undertakings. The 1956 industrial Policy Resolution added some more industries to the list. The original thinking was that as far as the public sector was concerned, it should enter fields where private sector would find it difficult to invest. By 1956, this had changed to an absolute preference for state ownership of industries and the public sector was supposed to capture the commanding heights of the economy.

Industrial production grew by 9.7 per cent in the first seven months of 1996—97, 1.9 percentage points slower than the 11.7 per cent growth in the first seven months of the previous year, which was the highest in 25 years. The growth of 9.5 to 10.5 per cent would still be the second highest growth rate in 25 years. It says, "the good performance of industrial production in 1996—97 is due entirely to the manufacturing sector, which has maintained its high growth." During the first seven months of the year the rate of growth of the manufacturing sector was 12.1 per cent, virtually the same as 12.3 per cent in 1995—96.

The Survey attributes the slowing of industrial production to the dramatic fall in the rate of growth of electricity production and a slowing down of growth in the mining sector, mainly because of the 10 per cent decline in crude oil production. During the first seven months of the year, electricity production has grown only by 3.4 per cent compared to 10.1 per cent in the corresponding period of 1995—96. If despite slowdown of electricity generation, manufacturing has recorded good growth, one possible reason could be captive generation, which is increasingly being used as a backup to public supply, the Survey adds. This hypothesis is supported by the growth of about 22 per cent in the volume of diesel imports.

Another noteworthy aspect of industrial production in 1996—97 has been acceleration in the rate of growth of capital goods production to 16.5 per cent from 15 per cent in the first seven months of the previous year. In contrast capital goods inports have declined by six per cent in the first seven months of the year. This according to the Survey, shows the increased competitiveness of the domestic capital goods industry.

The Survey also refers to the deceleration in the growth rate in the production of consumer durables, such as cars, to 9.8 per cent in the first seven months of 1996—97, compared to 30.2 per cent in the first seven months of the previous year. The delisensing of investment in consumer durable and decontrol of imports of parts of these goods, contributed to boom in investment and production in the sector. The decline in growth during 1996—97 suggests that the pent—up demand in the domestic economy has been met. Further growth will depend on increased cost competitiveness, which requires fuller exploitation of the comparative advantage that India has in the production of labour—intensive parts. Some analysts, however, seen in the sudden saturation of the demand a falacy in the general belief of the size of the middle class with good purchasing power, estimated at 200 million.

The Survey rates as poor the overall performance of the core and infrastructure sectors during the first 8 months of 1996—97 (April—November). Six industries, namely electricity generation, coal, steel, crude oil, petroleum products and cement, with a combined weight of 28.8 per cent in the Index of Industrial Production (IIP), averaged a growth of 4.1 poer cent in April—November, 1995. It says the previous Surveys had emphasised the need to accelerate, widen and deepen reforms of th non—tradable infrastructure and energy sectors, to avert an impending mismatch between economic growth and provision of these services. The new government, it says has repeatedly stressed its firm determination to reform the infrastructure and energy sectors and has take a number of policy decisions and new initiatives.

The Survey says continuing restraint on money supply growth is among the factors that have kept the prices in check. Despite the recent rising trend inthe growth of WPI, the average inflation for 1996—97 is expected to be at least one percentage point less than the average inflation in the previous year. There was complete change in the sectoral pattern of price changes du;ring 1996—97. The annual rate of inflation accelerated sharply in the "fuel, power, light and lubricants" and primary articles, while decelerating in the "manufactures" group. The annual rate of price increase in the fuel—power group went up to 17.4 per cent in January 1997 from 1.1 per cent a year ago because of administered price increase, while that of primary articles to 11.7 per cent from 2.6 per cent. The rate of growth in prices of manufactured goods declined to 3.6 poer cent from 6.9 per cent in the previous year. The rise in prices of primary goods has largely been due to rise in prices of cereals and fruits and vegetables.

Money supply growth has been higher in 1996—97 than in 1995—96, the Survey says, adding "Upto the fornight ended January 17, 1997, broad money (M3) grew by 10.6 per cent as against 8.2 per cent growth in the corresponding period of 1995—96. The average call money rate declined from a high of 13.75 per cent at the beginning of the currently financial year to a range of 5 to 11 per cent in September 1996 and ruled between 10 and 11 per cent in December 1996, before falling to low single digits in January 1997. The reversal of the 1997—96 excess demand for funds for investment in 1996–97 has led to a general softening of interest rates during the year. The cut—off yields on 91—day treasury bills has come down from 12.4 per cent in the first week of July to around 7.5 per cent at the end of January 1997.

Control over fiscal deficit was identified by the Update to the Economic Survey, presented by the United

Front Government last year as one of the three challenges for economicpolicy. The Budget for 1996—97 envisaged a reduction of the fiscal dificit by 0.8 per cent of GDP to 5 per cent from 5.8 per cent in 1995—96 (RE). The primary deficit is also budgeted to fall from 1.1 poer cent of GDP to 0.2 per cent, while the revenue deficit to 2.5 per cent of GDP from 3 per cent in 1995—96.

The reduction in fiscal deficit has been attempted through an increase in revenues coupled with a reduction in expenditure. Revenue receipts (net) are budgeted to increase by 18.3 per cent during 1996—97 (BE). Despite a larger outgo on account of interest payments, subsidies and provision for revision of salaries and pension, total revenue expenditure is budgeted to grow at a lower rate of 12.7 per cent compared to 17.5 per cent in the previously year (RE). This deceleration in the growth of revenue expenditure has led to a decline in revenue expenditure to GDP ratio from 13.1 per cent in 1995—96 to 12.9 per cent in 1996—97 (BE). This favourable outcome, the Survey claims, is largely on account of containment of non—interest, non—plan expenditure growth at 9.3 per cent during 1996—97, about half the growth of 18.6 per cent in 1995—96 (RE). Consequently, non–interest revenue expenditure as a proportion of GDP is budgeted to fall to 8.1 per cent from 8.3 per cent in 1996—97 (RE). The revenue deficit is budgeted to fall by 0.5 per cent point of GDP. One may, however, note that the comparison of Budget estimates (BE) with Revenue Estimates (RE) is not very realistic.

Public sector

Since Independence, the public sector in India has been guided by the Industrial Policy Resolution of 1956, which had as its objectives the acceleration of the rate of economic growth and speeding up of the industrialisation as means of achieving the socialistic pattern of society. Since in the initial phase of industrialisation, the capital was scare, the state sector assumed the predominance and direct responsibility for industrial development. The size of public sector in India is indeed very large. It includes government departments and its compaines whether in the Central or state sector, irrigation and power projects, railways, posts and telegraphs, ordnance factories and other departmental undertakings, banking, insurance, financial and other services. The focus here is however, on the Central public sector enterprises established as Government companies or statutory corporations excluding banking units.

After the initial exuberance of public sector entering into new areas of industrial manufacturing, providing technical services, trading, financial and services sectors, the public enterprises started facing various problems, some of these problems were due to historical reasons, while others were related to poor project management, over-manning, obsolete technology, poor order book positions etc. All these put together, the public sector as a whole started showing results far below the desired level in comparison to the investments made in them.

The Government announced a new Industrial Policy on 24 July 1991 which envisages liberalisation, competitive environment. The new Policy has laid down certain specific areas in respect of the public enterprises which are to be emphasized in order to make them better performers and more competitive. The slient features of the new Industrial Policy on the Public Sector are: (i) Portfolio of public sector investments will be reviewed with a veiw to focus the public sector on strategic, high-tech and essential infrastructure. Whereas some reservation for the public sector is being retained, there would be no bar for area exclusively to be opened up to the private sector selectively. Similarly, the public sector will also be allowed entry in areas not reserved for it; (ii)

Public enterprises which are chronically sick and which are unlikely to be turned around will for the formulation of revival, rehabilitation schemes, be referred to the Board for Industrial and Financial Reconstruction (BIFR), or other similar high level institutions created for the purpose. A social security mechanism will be created to protect the interest of workers likely to be affected by such rehabilitation packages; (iii) in order to raise resources and encourage wider public participation, a part of the governement's share-holding in the public sector would be offered to mutual funds, financial institutions, general public and workers; (iv) Boards of public sector companies would be made more professional and given greater powers; (v) there will be a greater thrust on performance improvement through the Memoranda of Understanding (MOU) system through which management would be granted greater autonomy and will be held accountable. Technical expertise on the part of the Goernment would be upgraded to make the MOU negotiations and implementation more effective; and (vi) to facilitate a fuller discussion on performance, the MOU singed between Government and the public enterprise would be placed in Parliament. While focussing on major management issues, this would also help place matters on day to day operations of public enterprises in their perspective.

As a major step for implementation of the Policy, the Government of India has disinvested varying percentage of its share-holdings in some PSUs. So far, the shares of 39 PSUs, have been disinvested in favour of the financial institutions, mutual funds, banks, foreign institutional investors and the public (PSUs-wise percentage Central Government holdings is shown in Table 1). This resulted in disinvestment of 152.07 crore share in 39 public sector undertakings and a sum of Rs. 9,794 crore was realised.

The shares of these companies are now listed on the stock exchanges. The valuation of the equity of these enterprises on the stock exchanges reflects the preceptions of the public in general and investors in particular of the performance and the expectations of the public from these enterprises. Besides, the Government has also offered a part of its equity holdings in some of these enterprises in favour of the employees, in order to encourage the employees participation in the managements a sence of commitment and belonging to an enterprise.

Over a period of time, the public enterprises have been faced with the chronical sickness and mounting losses. In the case of some of the enterprises, which have incurred huge losses and had eroded their networth, in order to formulate the revival/rehabilitation packages, a number of these enterprises have been referred to the Board for Industrial and Financial Reconstruction (BIFR). So far, 54 sick enterprises have been referred to BIFR for revival/rehabilitation. BIFR makes an independent assessment of the viability or otherwise of a particular enterprise afte keeping in the view points of the owner (Government), the employees, the financial institutions and the other concerned. Under the new Industrial Policy, greater thrust has been laid on the evaluation of the performance, through the system of MOUs which has also started yielding positive results in the form of better performance from the public enterprises.

There has been appreciable growth in the investments in the public sector over the years. In 1951, the investment in five Central Public Sector was Rs. 29 crore. This investment has gone up to Rs. 147,587 crore in 245 enterprises as on 31 March 1993 and at Rs. 164,332 crore in 246 enterprises in 1993-94. Thus, during 1993-94, the investment in public sector has increased by Rs.

16,745 crore registering an increase of 11.35 per cent. The overall financial performance of the manufacturing and service group enterprises for the last two years is given in table 2.

Public sector has been playing a dominant role in the fertilizer industry. The first state-owned fertilizer unit was set up in 1951 at Sindri in Bihar, which was followed by another plant at Nangal in Punjab. With the coming up of another fertilizer plant at Trombay, Government decided to bring all the public sector fertilizer units under the management of a single undertaking and the Fertilizer Corporation of India Limited (FCI) was accordingly incorporated in January 1961. The National Fertilizers Limited was established on 23 August 1974. Thereafter, the Fertilizer Corporation of India and the National Fertilizers Limited were re-organised into four companies on the basis of feedstock used and geographical considerations from 1 April 1978. At present, there are nine public sector undertakings under the administrative control of Department of Fertilizers. FCI has now four units, one each at Sindri (Bihar), Gorakhpur (U.P.) Talcher (Orissa) and Ramagundam (Andhra Pradesh), with a total installed capacity of 5.87 lakh tonnes of nitrogen. The National Fertilizers Limited (NFL) has, at present, five operating units, viz., the calcium ammonium nitrate plant at Nanagal and the urea plants at Nanagal, Bhatinda, Panipat and Vijaipur. With the commissioning of the Vijaipur plant in 1987-88, the total installed capacity of NFL has gone up to 10.36 lakh MT of nitrogen, making NFL the largest producer of nitrogenous fertilizers in the country. The Fertilizers and Chemicals Travancore Limited (FACT), Udyogamandal (Kerala), has, at present, three operating units, one at Udyogamandal and two at Cochin. Besides fertilizers, the company is engaged in the manufacture of chemicals.

With the commissioning of caprolactum plant in October 1990, the company has entered the field of petro-chemicals also. FACT Engineering and Design Organisation (FEDO), another division of the company is engaged in design, engineering, procurement, supervision of construction and commissioning of fertilizers/chemical plants.

Rashtriya Chemicals and Fertilizers Limited (RCF) is in charge of the Trombay plants and the large gas-based fertilizer plant at Thal which started commercial production in 1985. Hindustan Fertilizer Corporation Limited has five units in production, three at Namrup in Assam and one each at Durgapur in West Bengal and Barauni in Bihar, having total annual installed capacity of 6.54 lakh tonnes of nitrogen. Madras Fertilizers Limited (MFL) is a joint venture, with the Government of India holding 67.55 per cent of the equity share capital and the National Iranian Oil Company holding the remaining 32.45 per cent. The annual installed capacity of MFL is 1.76 lakh tonnes of nitrogen and 1.12 lakh tonnes of phosphate. Pyrites, Phosphates and Chemicals Limited (PPCL), set up in March 1960, is presently engaged in the exploration of pyrites deposits as well as production of single super phosphate at Amjhore in Bihar, exploration-cumproduction mining of pyrites deposits at Saladipura in Rajasthan and mining of rock phosphate ore from the Mussuoorie phosphorite deposits.

Projects and Development India Limited (PDIL), formerly known as Fertilizer (Planning & Development) India Limited, is engaged in design, engineering, procurement and supervision of construction/ commissioning of fertilizer and allied chemical plants. The company has played a pioneering role in developing, entirely on its own initiative, the know-how for manufacture of catalysts in India. Pradeep Phosphates

L:imited (PPL) was established in December, 1981 for setting up a phosphatic fertilizer complex at Paradeep in Orissa. Phase-I of the project, comprising 7.20 lakh TAP capacity DAP plant and allied facilities was commissioned in 1986. Phase-II of the project, comprising sulphuric acid and phosphoric acid plants, also went into commercial production in June 1992.

Indian Farmers Fertilizer Cooperative Limited (IFFCO) incrporated in 1975 and Krishak Bharati Cooperative Limited (KRIBHCO) incorporated in 1985, are the two cooperative sector undertakings under the administrative control of the Department of Fertilizers. IFFCO has four operating units, one each at Kalol and Kandla in Gujarat and Phulpur and Aonla in Uttar Pradesh. KRIBHCO has a gas-based urea-ammonia plant at Hazira in Gujarat with a capacity to produce 14.50 lakh tonnes of urea per annum. The combined installed capacity of IFFCO and KRIBHCO is 15.31 lakh tonnes of nitrogen and 3.09 lakh tonnes of phosphate.

The assumption on the savings front is that the public sector would be able to return positive savings to the tune of 2.8 per cent of GDP. Currently, the net dissavings in the government sector in in the order of one and-a-half per cent, while the public secor undertakings return positive savings, amounting to a little over three and-a-half per cent GDP. However, the scope for the latter to increase further is limited, as the share of public sector units' (PSUs) output in the GDP gradually declines in the wake of reforms that seek to confer a larger role to private capital. In fact, it would not be surprising if the PSU savings as percentage of GDP actually came down. With public sector saving at 2.8 per cent of GDP, the government (both at the Centre and the States) needs to bring down their dissavings substantially. It implies a substantial curb on profligacy sundrome, further fiscal consolidation and an impressive step-up in tax revenues.

The Ninth Plan of Rs. 27.2 lakh crore at 1996-97 base prices would have about 40 per cent of the resources allocated for the public sector. This would include Rs. 3.76 lakh crore as budgetary support. But then, growth is not just a question of gross investment—its sectoral distribution as also the policies that direct it are equally relevant. And, it is here that the government holds the key entirely. In fact, any particular level of budgetary support to the Plan makes little sense without refernce to its sectoral allocation. Budget funds are required to meet the investment needs of sectors that will not attract private funds, particularly the social sectors. The government must, therefore, first prioritze the sectors and then discuss the amount it would invest during the Plan period.

While raising resources would be the major problem during the Ninth Plan period, the Centre and the States wouls have to increase tax rates, remove the loopholes in tax laws and improve collection. There is need for steps by the Centre and the States to increase tax-GDP ratio for additional resource mobilization. The suggestion made by the West Bengal Chief Minister, Mr. Jyoti Basu, for tapping black money sources to raise resources and to ensure that people having black money are forced to part with a slice of their ill-gotten wealth for developmental purposes is worth considering.

Reforms

Among the various policies enunciated for restructuring of the PSUs, a major step involved the disinvestment of a part of Government equities in selected public undertakings for improving their performance as well as to increase their public accountability by broad basing their management and ownership. In the process of disinvestment, a major step taken by the government has been to set up the Disinvestment Commission for working out the terms and conditions as well as modalities pertaining to disinvestment of public equities. At present the government contemplates restructuring of equity in 40 major PSUs, including blue-chip companies like ONGC, GAIL, SAIL, MTNL, IPCL, NTPC, BEML, Power Grid, NHPC, IOC, IBP and Bongalgoan Refineries. While the Commission is to determine the modalities of disinvestment, the actual sale of PSU shares would be done through Deptt. of Public Enterprises (DPE). The Commission also intends to identify the non-core PSUs where the Government may even disinvest by more than 50 per cent and may have minority ownership.

Under auspices of the National Renewal Fund (NRF) set up in February 1992, for mobilising funds to assist voluntary retired persons from PSUs in undergoing re-training and re-deployment, Rs. 252 crore and Rs. 217 crore were released in 1994-95 and 1995-96, respectively. An estimated number of 87,800 workers have opted for voluntary retirement so far and a major portion of NRF has been utilised in the textile sector.

Indistrial relations have shown a steady improvement in the years follow the economic reforms. Mandays lost due to strikes and lockouts declined significantly from 22.97 million in 1992-93 to 17.99 million in 1995-96. This was mainly due to improvement in the industrial relations situation in cotton, engineering, coal and non-coal mining, beverages, tobacco & tobacco products, jute and rubber industries. During 1992-96, industrial unrest was witnessed mainly in the states of Andhra Pradesh, Gujarat, Tamil Nadu and Maharashtra, Government's proactive role through timely and effective conciliation of industrial disputes and involvement of the social partners in the formulation and implementation of labour and industrial relations policies and programmes has successfully harmonised the interests of employers and workers.

Corporate sector

First company legislation in India was an Act for registration of joint stock companies enacted in 1850. This was followed by the Companies Act, 1913. As a result of recommendations of a committee under the chairmanship of C.H. Bhabha to make suggestions for company law reform, the Companies Act, 1956 was enacted as a Central lefislation. Prior to enactment of this Act, administration of companies' legislation was the responsibility of the state governments.

The Companies Act, 1956 has been in force for the last 38 years and during this period it has been amended over 16 times. Amendments of 1969, 1974, 1977 and 1988 are of special importance. By the amendment Act of 1969, system of appointing managing agencies or secretaries or treasurers in companies was abolished. Under the 1974 amendment, powers of High Court relating to certain sections of the Companies Act were transferred to Company Law Board. Scope of Section 43A was enlarged so as to treat large private limited companies as deemed public limited companies. A new Section 58A was inserted to regulate acceptance of deposits by companies. Section 108A to Section 108H were introduced to check take-over bids by large groups.

The 1977 amendment inserted, inter alia Section 634A enabling Company Law Board to enforce its orders under Section 17, 18, 19, 79 141 and 186 of the Act as a decree of a court of law. The Companies Act, 1956 provides various powers to Central Government and Company Law Board, to monitor, regulate and control the affairs of companies. Salient features of the 1988 amendments are: (a) setting up of an independent Company Law Board to exercise such judicial and quasi-judicial functions as are presently being exercised either by Court or Central government and proposed to be transferred to that Board; (b) dispensing with Government approval for managerial appointments and remuneration, subject to fulfilment of certain statutory guidelines which are proposed to be incorporated in the Act itself; (c) delinking of rates of depreciation from rates specified under the Income Tax Act and laying down rates of depreciation in the Act itself to reflect true and fair view of the state of affairs of the company; (d) protecting the interest of investors by providing for intervention by Company Law Board against non-payment of public deposits and certain other matters, compulsory redemption of preference shares in certain cases, requiring companies to disclose reasons for refusal to register transfer of shares, protecting the rights of thee transfere pending mutation of his name in the register of members, and also compulsory lilsting of all public issues; (e) reducing unnecessary cost or burden by requiring companies to attach only an abridged version * for disclosure of information relating to conservation of energy, technology absorption, foreign exchange earnings and outgo as well as particulars of employees having some minimum stake in the company and drawing remuneration in excess of that drawn by managerial personnel.

The number of joint stock companies, both Government and non-Government incorporated under the Companies Act, 1956 and at work in India as on 31 March 1994 was 3,08,324. Of these 3,05,625 were limited by shares, 349 with unlimited liability and 2,350 were limited by guarantee or were associations not for profit.

The 3,05,625 companies limited by shares have paid up capital of Rs. 1,04,890.8 crore. These comprised 38,000 public limited companies and 2,67,625 private limited companies with paid up capital of Rs. 70,112.1 and Rs. 34,778.7 crore respectively.

New registrations

During 1993-94, 30,393 companies were registered under the Companies Act. These include 18 Government companies and 30,273 non-government companies with liability limited by shares, 13 non-government companies with unlimited liability and 89 non-government companies with liability limited by guarantee and associations not for profit.

Of the 30,291 companies limited by shares registered during the year, 3,625 were public limited companies with an aggregate authorised capital of Rs. 5,456.2 crore and 26,666 were private limited companies with an aggregate authorised capital of Rs. 3,152.1 crore.

New capital issue

Section 60 of the Companies Act requires that prospectuses issued by or on behalf of the companies or in relation to an intended company inviting offers from the public for the subscription or purchase of any shares or debentures be delivered to the Registrar of Companies for registration. Section 67(3) provides that if the offer or invitation can properly be regarded as not being calculated to result, directly or indirectly, in the shares or debentures becoming available for subscription or purchase by persons other than those receiving offer or inviation, as being of a domestic concern of the persons making or receivinng such offer or invitation, shall not be treated as made to the public. Thus, prospectuses for issue of shares or debentures by private placement are not required to be registered with the Registrar of

Companies. During the year ending 31 March 1994, 525 non government, non-financial public limited companies delivered to the Registrar of Companies for registration, the copies of prospectuses under Section 60 of the Act raising an amount of Rs. 7,952.8 crore from public as against 426 prospectuses delivered by the companies in the previous year for raising an amount of Rs. 6,331.1 crore. Of the 525 companies which issued prospectuses during 1993-94, 494 companies (or 94 per cent) invited applications for equity share capital, of the remaining 31 companies, invited applications for equity shares as well as debentures and 27 for debentures only.

Of the total amount of Rs. 7,952.8 crore issued through prospectuses during 1993-94, Rs. 3,542.7 crore (44.5 per cent approximately) was in respect of equity shares, Rs. 4,386.1 crore (55.1 per cent approximately) for debentures and balance of Rs. 24 crore (0.3 per cent) in respect of preference shares capital amounting to Rs. 4,310.7 crore or 54.2 per cent of the total amount covered by the prsopectuses, was offered to the public and balance of Rs. 3,642.1 crore or 45.8 per cent was earmarked for firm allotment to the promoters, directors, existing shareholders and employees of the companies, non-resident Indians, financial institutions, banks and the state industrial development corporations.

During 1993-94, 259 companies went into liquidation or otherwise became defunct or ceased to work and were struck off under Section 560 (5) of the Companies Act, 1956.

Small and tiny enterprises

The primary objective of the Government's policy for Small and Tiny Enterprises would be to impart more vitality and growth impetus to the sector to enable it to contribute its mite fully to the economy particularly in terms of out put, employment and exports. In this context, it is heartening to note that at the end of the 7th Plan period the small scale sector accounted for meariy 35 per cent of the gross value of the out put in the manufacturing sector and over 40 per cent of the total exports from the country. It also provided employment opportunties to around 12 million people. To ensure the growth of the Small and Tiny sector the Government proposes to review and modify all Statutes, regulations and procedures wherever necessary, to ensure that their operations do not militate against the interest of small and village enterprises.

As mentioned earlier in this paper, manufacturing units with an investment and plant and machinery up to 75 lakhs and units which are willing to undertake an export obligation to the extent of 30 per cent of their annual production by 3rd year with an investment of Rs. up to 75 lakhs are eligigle for small scale registration. The investment limit in respect of Tiny Enterprises has been increased from Rs. 2 lakhs to Rs. 5 lakhs. With the objective of providing support to the service sector in view of its potential for generating employment, it has been decided that in future all industry related service and business enterprises irrespective of their location would be recognised as small scale industries and their investment ceiling would correspond to those of Tiny Enterprises.

Units in the small scale sector (other than Tiny Enterprises) would be entitled to benefits like preference in land allocation, power connection, access to facilities for skill/technology upradation. Tiny enterprises would in addition to these benefits will also be eligble for additional support including easier access to institutional finance, priority in the Government purchase programme and relaxation from certain provisions of labour laws.

Inadequate access to credit-both short—term and long—term remains a perennial problem facing the small scale sector. Emphasis would henceforth shift from subsidiese/cheap credit, except for specified target groups, and efforts would be made to ensure both adequate flow of credit on a normative basis, and the quality of its delivery, for viable operations of this sector. A special monitoring agency would be set up to oversee that the genuine credit needs of the small scale sector are fully met. To provide access to the capital market and to encourage modernisation and technlogical upgradation, it has been decided to allow equity participation by other industrial undertakings in the SSI, not exceeding 24 per cent of the total shareholding. this would also provide a powerful boost to ancillarisation and subcontracting, leading to expansion of employment opportunities.

Regulatory provisions relating to the management of private limited companies are being liberalised. A Limited Partnership Act will be introduced to enhance the supply of risk capital to the small scale sector. Such an Act would limit the financial liability of the new and non-active partners/entrepreneurs to the capital invested.

A beginning has been made towards solving the problems of delayed payments to small industries by setting up of factoring services through Small Industries Development Bank of India (SIDBI). Network of such services would be set up throughout the country and operated through commercial banks. A suitable legislation will be introduced to ensure prompt payment of small industries' bills.

To facilitate location of industries in rural/backward areas and to promote stringer linkages between agriculture and industry, a new Scheme of Integrated Infrastructural Develpoment (including Technological Back-up Services) for Small Scale Industries would be implemented with the active participation of State Government and Financial Institutions. A beginning in this direction will be made this year itself.

A Technology Development Cell (TDC) would be set up in the Small Industries Development Organisation (SIDO) which would provide technology inputs to improve productivity and competitiveness of the products of the small scale sector. The TDC would coordinate the activities of the Tool Rooms, Process-cum-Product Development Centres (PPDCs), existing as well as to be established under SIDO, and would also interact with the other industrial research and development organisations to achieve its objectives.

Adequacy and equitable distribution of indigenous and imported raw material would be ensured to the small scale sector, particularly the tiny sub-sector. Policies would be so designed that they dc not militate against entry of new units. Based on the capacity needs, Tiny/ Small Scale Units would be given priority in allocation of indigenous raw materials.

A proper and adequate arrangement for delivery of total package of incentives and services at the District level will be evolved and implemented.

Inspite of the vast domestic market, marketing remains a problem area for Small and Tiny Enterprises. Mass consumption labour intensive products are predominantly being marketed by the organised sector. The Tiny/Small Scale Sector will be enabled to access existing support mechanism. Market promotion would be undertaken through cooperative/public sector institutions, other specialised/professional marketing agencies and consortia approach, backed up by such incentives as considered necessary.

National Small Industries Corporation (NSIC) would

concentrate on marketing of mass consumption items under common brand name and organic links between NSCI and State Small Industries Development Corporations (SSIDCs) would be established.

Government recognises the need to widen and deepen complementarity in production programmes of large/medium and small industrial sectors. Parts, components, sub assemblies, etc. required by large public/private sector undertakings would be encouraged for production in a techno-economically viable manner through small scale ancillary units. Industry associations would be encouraged to establish subcontracting exchanges, in addition to strengthening the existing ones under the SIDO. Emphasis would also be laid on promotion of a viable and competitive component market.

Though the small scale sector is making significant contribution to total exports both direct and indirect, a large potential remains untapped. SIDO has been recognised as the nodal agency to support the small scale industries in export promotion. An Export Development Centre would be set up in SIDO to serve the small scale industries through its network of field offices to further augment export activities of this sector.

A greater degree of awareness to produce goods and services conforming to national and international standards would be created among the small scale sector.

Industry Associations would be encouraged and supported to establish quality counselling and common testing facilities. Technology Informaton Centres to provide updated knowledge on technology and markets would be established.

Where non-conformity with quality and standards involves risk to human life and public health, compulsory quality control would be enforced.

Are-oriented programme of modernisation and technological upgradation aimed at improving productivity, efficiency and cost effectiveness in the small scale sector would be pursued. Specific industries in large concentrations/clusters would be identified for studies in conjunction with SIDBI and other banks. Such studies will establish commercial viability of modernisation prescriptions, and financial support would be provided for modernisation of these industries on a priority basis.

Indian Institutes of Technology (IITs) and selected Regional/other Engineering Colleges will serve as Technological Information, design and Development Centres in their respective command areas.

Government will continue to support first generation entrepreneurs thrugh training and other measures. Large number of EDP trainers and motivators will be trained to significantly expand the Entrepreneurship Development Programmes (EDP). Industry Associations would also be encouraged to participate in this venture effectively.

EDP would be built into the curricula of vocational and other degree level courses.

Women entrepreneurs will receive support through special training programmes. Definition of "Women Enterprises" would be simplified. The present stipulation regarding employment of majority of women workers would be dispensed with and units in which women entrepreneurs have majority shareholding and management control, would be defined as "Women Enterprises".

Additional employment opportunities would be generated through training of multi-disciplinary barefoot managers to suit special requirements of the small scale sector.

The persistent complaint of small scale units of being subjected to a large number of Acts and Laws, being required to maintain a number of registers and submit returns, and face an army of inspectors, would be attended to within a specified time frame of three months.

Procedures would be simplified, bureaucratic controls effectively reduced, unnecessary interference eliminated an paper work cut down to the minimumto enable the entrepreneur to concentrate on production and marketing function.

The Government has also announced a number of steps for promoting Handloom sector, handicrafts sector and other village industries.

Technical advice and assistance to small scale manufacturers is provided by the Small Industries Development Organisation through its network of 16 service institutes, 16 branch institutes, 58 extension, production and training centres. The organisation also provides common service and tool room facilities in workshops attached to small industries, service institutes and extension centres. It conducts courses in management and technical disciplines. During 1974-75, it provided technical assistance to 1,02,684 entrepreneurs and visited 70,965 factories for spot guidance.

Two new centres namely the Central Insititute of Tool Design, Hyderabad, and The Institute for Design of Electrical Measuring Instruments, Bombay, have started providing technical guidance and training for entrepreneurs.

The National Small Industries Corporation, which was set up in 1955, operates the scheme of procuring machinery for small-scale manufacturers on a hire-purchase basis on concessional terms. The value of machines delivered under this scheme during the period April-October 1974 was Rs. 5.69 crores as against Rs. 3.25 crores during the corresponding period of the previous year. It also assists the small-scale sector in processing orders from government departments and agencies. The value of stores purchased by the Directorate General of Supply and Disposals from April to November 1974 was about Rs. 37 crores. The Prototype Development and Training Centres set up with American, West German and Japanese assistance at Rajkot, Okhla (Delhi) and Howrah impart training to persons engaged in small-scale industries.

Specialised agencies

Hitherto the emphasis was minly on agro-based industries. The growth of these industries was no doubt important for providing a ready market to the agricultural outputs, to create employment opportunities in view of seasonal nature of agriculture and to stabilise the farmer's income. Several specialised agencies such as the State Finance Corporations, Small Scale Reserve Bank, and the various technical guidance and assistance schemes of the Central Government, State Governments, Reserve Bank and State Bank of India were directed mainly to sustain the growth of small scale and cottage industries.

It was, however, realised at a later stage that the institutional at the "output" end is only one part of the game. Indian agriculture does not face any serious problem from the demand side. It is with the improvement in the technique of production that the cost of farming can be reduced and the productivity of the land can be improved in order to meet ever growing demand of agricultural outpout from direct consumers as well as from industries. The institutional set-up was, therefore, geared up to discover means for improving the technique of agricultural production and also to manufacture agriculture machinery.

At the highest level various agricultural research centres, headed by Indian Council of Agriculture Research, are performing important functions in the development and distribution of scientific knowledge of agriculture. There is also the Indian Society of Agriculture Engineers which provides a wealth of information for the application of science and technology to farming. At the village level cooperative societies are propagating and, where possible, implementing, the programmes of the research centres.

Cooperative societies and various official organisations have performed important functions but because of their limitations, these agencies could not meet the requirements of mechanised agriculture which has recetly gained importance for improving agricultural productivity.

Thus with a view to meeting the rapidly growing demand of farmers for standard agricultural machinery equipment, e.g., tractors, power tillers, power threshers, seed-cum-fertilisers, drills, power sprayers and dusters, diesel and electric pump-sets, on cash or hire-purchase basis, the State Agro-Industrial Corporations have been established by the Government.

These corporation have been established in almost all the states. They are performing multifarious activities connected with not only the supply of agricultural machinery but also providing credit for the purpose. Some of them have ambitious programmes of designing and assembling tractors and manufacturing various tools and implements. But in fairness to the Corporations it must be recorded that none of them is more than three years old. What is more, some of them have the right ideas. In Gujarat, for instance, the AIC has decided to accord priority to the setting up of new cold storage plants in Banaskantha and Balsar, Onion dehydration plants at Jamnagar and Bhavnagar and hydrogenated oil unit in the Saurashtra region. In West Bengal, the AIC will supply diesel pumping sets to poor farmers owning two to five acres of land on payment of Rs. 70 cash down, the balance of the price–Rs. 3,500–being recoverable in easy instanlments. In Tamil Nadu the AIC is not only going into the processing and marketing of farm produce but will also set up factories for the servicing and repair of the 1,000 new tractors which are sold in the state every year.

It is evidnt that the growth of agro-industries cannot reverse the process of urbanisation. Most of the plants for processing farm products or "waste" materials released by the existing agro-based industries like textiles must be established near the consuming centres if they are to pave their way. All that can be done in the circumstances is to establish new industrial units, both big and small, in district towns and away from the major cities. Any effort to confine the new agro-industries to the rural or semi-urban areas is bound to hinder their growth and will in the end be self-defeating.

Since there are quite a number of common problems which these institutions are likely to face, it might be worthwhile to establish a Central Agro-Industrial Corporation of India to coordinate the work of these state institutions. Besides coordinating the working of the state corporations, the central organisation can be entrusted with research and development of technology. Centralisation of research will eliminate waste and duplication. The State Corporations will, however, continue to collect data rom their regional offices to make them available to the central organisation. It will also be

the task of the cental agency to arrange the production of different components of machinery and implements in different areas according to the local facilities available on the "comparative cost" basis. The proposed corporation can also serve as an effective agency in arranging the colllection of technical knowledge from abroad and distribution of imported machinery.

The massive expenditure that the Government has incurred on agricultural development has in one way or another gone to prop up a new rich class by passing millions of small farmers and landless labourers. There are growing indications of discontent among those who have found the cost of acquiring modern equipment and agricultural inputs soaring, on the one hand, and official and somehow getting channelled away from them, on the other.

The Government's decision to establish 500 pilot agro-service centres in the country is a step in the right direction. The programme is being jointly sponsored by the Ministry of Agriculture and the Ministry of Industrial Development and is designed to provide a wide range of services from custom-hiring of tractors and other farm equiptment and repair and maintenance of agricultural machinery to soil testing, crop spraying, water anaylsis and land and field services such as levelling and contour surveying. The scheme is intended to provide employment in the rural area as well as to accelerate the process of modernisation in the villages. It is particularly aimed at providing help to the small farmers and the weaker sections of the rural community in the relatively backward areas. The rapid increase in the use of tractors, pumps, mechanical threshers and other machines, not to speak of community radios, transistors and other personal gadgetry, has created a demand for easily available repair and maintenance facilities on a wide scale. Then agro-service centres can perform a valuable function provided they are suitably staffed and have the requisite managerial competence. The Government has negotiated World Bank assistance for tractor-cum-groundwater development projects in Punjab, Haryana and Tamil Nadu. Agro-service centres could be established alongside these programmes for a start.

As far as mechanical equipment like tractors and pumps are concerned, it would be most' desirable for the country to standardise on a few broad categories (not necessarily makes) so that problems of maintenance and the stocking of parts and components are not needlessly complicated by type differences. Little thought appears to have been given to this matter so far. But it is obviously something that calls for an early policy consideration.

Education and ninth plan

Education is the lifeline of development, be it spiritual or economic, scientific or technological, national or global. In the 21st century, countries will be measured by the education and health status of their population and not by GDPs and GNPs. The foremost component of education is its definition, aims, goals and objectives translated into an effective and practical policy. Included in this policy are a national curriculum, teaching strategies and evaluation procedures for measuring stated outcomes. Hence, an education policy and curriculum is to educational institutions what a blueprint is to an architect.

The education of an individual can be divided into five stages, namely preschool, primary, secondary, tertiary and adult education. The stage of preschool education is to the nation and educational institutions what a foundation is to a building. Both require a lot of specialization, knowledge and planning. Both are areas where we cannot afford to make a single mistake, else the entire structure will come tumbling down, or, we will have a scenario as highlighted they are both invisible. Further, just as a building can only be constructed with locally available materials, so too, a successful education policy and curriculum must reflect the culture, the needs, the norms, the language, and the values of its people.

Last but not least just as the construction of a building does not start from its roof, so too, there cannot be a downward extension of the education policy and curriculum. However, an examination of our education system over the length and breadth of the country, reflects just that! CBSE, ISC and IB (International Baccalaureate diploma) have become the focus and objective of our education system with an overdose of formal learning, texbooks, an overemphasis, on English language, an inappropriate age for admissions, and proliferation of private schools and teaching shops.

There are many problems with the Ministry's perception, namely:

— The most basic issue is that the new policy on education (NPE 1992) notwithstanding, the focus of our education system is CBSE, which neither prepares the children for life nor for the existing international competitive ethos—a point that MHRD has chosen to ignore. The problems as highlighted are an outcome of the deliberate ignorance of education by the MHRD in the past:

— As per National Council of Applied Economic Research (NCAER) report, excluding drop-outs, 55 million primary school children have never stepped into a school. Not only does it burgeon child labour statistics, these children and their parents know that the existing system does not prepare their children for life. So rejection of the system through child labour, and, poverty make for an excellent scapegoat. Instead of applying itself to the curriculum issues as highlighted by the Yashpal Committee report and advise the Planning Commission to make 'Education Policy' as the springboard to success, the MHRD has chosen to indulge in populist programmes like NSPE and DPEP.

— There has been a sharp rise in our interest payments and interest rates as highlighted. But the MHRD has chosen to borrow further from commercial international banks to fund a dead end UEE programme.

— The statutory transfer and enforcement of elementary education from the Directive Principles of the Constitution to Fundamental Human Right, will in all probability backfire. Instead of decentralizing power and placing it in the hands of the people, it has the capacity to further empower and strengthen the bureaucrats.

— Further, for the past 50 years, the government has demonstrated a stubborn lack of will to implement the Directive Principles of the Constitution. What is so sacrosanct about Fundamental Rights? Do we have a democratic education policy in place? Is the infrastructure in place? Do we have the required and trained human power, ready to take the plunge? Have the PRIs really placed the power into the hands of the 'real' people or is it still concentrated in the secretariats of the Union and State governments? Have we really reached the monitoring and supervision stage to dare statutory enforcement of primary education? Have we really dumped the frivolous and cantankerous educational issues into the Indian Ocean?

— There is a contradiction in allowing the corporate sector and private sector into primary education as well as making it free and compulsory through statutory enforcement.

— Last but not least is the issue of funding and finance. A glance at the primary education trend during the eight five year plans, and the continuous tussle at the State-level of financing primary education vs other sectors, it is a foregone conclusion that primary education will emerge a loser.

With the colossal expenditure just on incentives to attract students through midday meals, free textbooks and uniforms, and scores of other expensive programmes, a question on everybody's lips is: After all this expenditure and programmes, do the students learn anything? If so, what do they learn? Is the acquired information useful to them? Despite such heavy funding through borrowed and taxpayers' money and the numerous populist programmes, why are the dropout rates so high? What is the correcd message–privatization of primary education or free and compulsory primary education? How does the government explain 10 per cent of rural population attending private schools vs 2 per cent in 1986? Why are we spending so heavily on a dead-end adult education programme? How has the programme benefited them if during the VIII Plan unemployment and underemployment has increased while self-employment and salaried employment has declined.

If we want to outbeat the competitive ethos and emerge a winner without being a drain on the exchequer, the following suggestions need to be placed on the front burner:

— Define education, literacy and development such that the entire nation understands it, accepts it and fully embraces it.

— The focus of the education policy must shift from the 3 Rs to the 3 Hs, i.e. the head, heart and hand—an education policy towards self-reliance and self-employment. The way we have defined education, literacy and development, we are only trying to catch our shadows, knowing fully well that shadows cannot be caught.

— Justify the logic for transferring education and health to the sector—charity syndrome. Such segregation and compartmentalization only fuels deficits and inflation.

— Ours is the typical case of the candle burning upside down! It is indeed very sad that during the Ninth Plan, primary education is to be guided and pushed forward for achieving the 7 per cent growth rate against the NPE (1992) grain of separating jobs from education.

— The issue is not one of resource crunch but one of will power, imagination and magnanimity to shun the powers and material gains accrued through chairs. The issue is one of redefining our education policies, be it industry, agriculture, employment, etc. The issue is one of redefining our education policy so that rural-urban dichotomies, gender dichotomies, rich-poor dichotomies are reduced. The issue is one of having the will to implement the new policy. The issue is one of demonstrating flexibility and tolerance to other points of issue is one of shedding fear and hypocrisy.

It was Netaji Subhas Chandra Bose, who, in his Haripura presidential address in February 1938 gave birth to the concept of national planning. Later, in his address delivered at the Industries Ministers' Conference in Delhi on 2 October, 1938, he outlined his concept of national planning. On 19 October, 1938, he offered the chairmanship of National Planning Committee to Jawaharlal Nehru. In October 1946, a national level Advisory Planning Board was wet up. And in 1952, the Planning Commission was formed.

Since his Haripura address, Netaji had been stressing on industrialization, employment and education as the three springboards of national reconstruction. So had Gandhij, but with a different perspective and focus,with some convergence and overlapping. While Netaji was more inclined towards self-reliance through socialism, Gandhiji was inclined towards an indigenous model of education and capitalis. Neither views prevailed. Eventually, it was industrializaton, with neither a socialist nor capitalist ideology, that monopolized the first eight five year plans, accompanied with its positive and negative outcomes.

On 16 January, 1997 the National Development Council approved the Ninth Five Year Plan (1997-2002) approach paper, targeting a seven per cent economic growth. The Plan seeks growth with equity and distributive justice while focusing on agriculture and rural development as the means to provide employment and eradicate poverty. The target for agricultural growth is 4.5 per cent. The total Plan outlay proposes a 30 per cent increase over the VIII Plan outlay.

Ever since, the Plan has attracted immense criticism. But before discussing the Ninth Plan approach to education, a quich overview of the Ninth Plan framework is required.

Interestingly, in its introductory chapter, the plan is silent on the health sector. The preoccupation is with economics and the accompanying materialistic infrastructure at the cost of human capital. By clubbing education, health, family welfare, women and child development, housing, water supply and urban development under social sector, the Plan has deliberately chosen to inculcate and further the 'dependence-on-government' syndrome.

In the process, the Plan has attracted much flak, and rightly so, from the nation's intelligentsia, luminaries and common people. The criticism ranges from questioning the very significalce of the Planning Commission, to its methodology, to the finances and budgets.

Just to highlight a few comments, Mr. Jagmohan, MP, compares the Plan to a loose denture with blunt and uneven teeth. Columnist Shastri finds it fundmentally antagonistic to the liberalization ideology. And Mr. B.M. Bhatial, economic analyst has termed the entire approach as cavalier. Of course, the maximum criticism it has attracted is on the budgetary support and resources. With a budgetary outlay of Rs. 8,75,000 crore, bifurcated into a capital investment of Rs. 7,60,000 crore and a budgetary support of Rs. 3,70,000 crore, everything has been left to our imagination.

On the other hand, the biggest failure of the Plan has been to deliberately miss the 'education' boat for the ninth time. It took all of 50 years of our Independence for the contry's situation to be as highlighted. Simply, because our most learned planners refused to make an integrated, indigenous education policy as the springboard of national reconstruction.

Ninth plan and employment

In working out the size of the wage employment programmes, we have to ensure that at least one member of every family below the poverty line gets employment for a minimum of 100 days in a year to cover the seasonal unemployment. The 38th round of NSSO has estimated about 44 million families below the poverty line in rural areas (in 1983—84) and providing employment to one member each of such families for 100 days would requre employment generation of 4,400 million mandays. If we take the poverty estimates of the 43rd round of NSSO and average size of family as 4.5, there are about 30 million families who are below the poverty line. To provide 100 days of employment to one member of each family, 3,000 million mandays will be required. At present, abut 24 million persons have got themselves registered under EAS and this figure would go up as EAS will be implemented throughout the country (till October 1996, EAS was limited to 3,206 blocks only). The poor people seeking employment could roughly go up to 35 million or so, when EAS would be extended to the entire country in 1997—98. During the normal years, we, therefore, have to generate about 3,000—3,500 million mandays in a year to meet the assurance of 100 employment to all those rural poor who need and seek employment. At present, the weighted average minimum wage is about Rs. 30 per manday and taking into account the wage material ratio of 60:40, thecost of generation of one manday would be Rs. 50. For generation of 3,000—3,500 million mandays,l we would reqquire Rs. 15,000—16,500 crore every year. Given the resources, it may, however, not be possible for the Indian economy to support such a massive programme. But then, the implementation of the Maharashtra EGS show that all the poor may not turn up for the kind of work provided under wage employment programmes. The actual requirement of funds would be somewhat less than the projections above. The provision of Rs. 60,000 crore in the Ninth Plan for rural employment, the major portion of which would go to the wage employment programmes, should, therefore, be sufficient to take care of the lowest rung of poverty.

The wage employment programmes in India started from the experimentation/pilot phases, in the 1960s and the 70s and then consolidated in the 80s and are now moving towards a scenario which guarantees employment, although it is beyond the economic capacity of the Centre for the present. We are in the assurance kind of scenario, where the implementation of EAS would certainly mitigate the hardships of the poorest of the poor in the rural areas by providing employment and food security in terms of increased purchasing power and distribution of food grains. The point that the present wage employment programmes in India are based on the vast experiences of the implementation, would strengthen our optimism in the Ninth Plan in which we would be moving towards a full employment situation. It is also heartening to note that during the Ninth Plan, EAS along with JRY would become perhaps the largest wage employment programme of its kind anywhere in the world.

We are on the threshold of the Ninth Five Year Plan, where available indications are that Rs. 60,000 crore will be provided for rural employment and a major portion of this allocation will be going for the wage employment schemes like the Jawahar Rizgar Yojana (JRY) and the Employment Assurance Scheme (EAS). India lives in villages, where agriculture provides employment to about teo—thirds of the population. Agriculture, being seasonal in nature, cannot provide employment year round. The continuous increase in population worsened the unemployment problem in rural areas and the Indian economy has, therefore, always been in less than full employment situation, which itself experience seasonal agricultural peaks and troughs. There has always been a fap betweenf full employment situation and the actual availability of employment. This gap becomes worse in lean agricultural season and alarming during droughts and famine—like conditions. To bridge this gap, various wage employment programmes were launched by the Centre from time to time, like the Food for Work Programme (FWP) in 1977, the National Rural Employment Programme (NREP) in 1980, the Rural Landless Employment Gurantee Programme (RLEGP) in 1983, the Jawahar Rozgar Yojana (JRY) in 1989 and the Employment Assurance Scheme (EAS) in 1993.

The culmination of earlier experiences of the implementation of wage employment programmes was the Food for Work Programme (FWP) which was started as a non—plan scheme to augment the funds of State governments for maintenance of public works on which large investment had been made in the past by utilizing available stocks of food grains. There were, however, lot of expectations from the programme but is did not make much headway in the beginning due to certain constraints inherent in the scheme itself.

On review of this programme and the dificulties experienced by the States, the scheme was liberalized to include all ongoing plan non—plan works and new items of public and community works. The basic objectives of FWP were to generate additional gainful employment for unemployed and underemployed persons in the rural areas and to improve the incomes and nutritional levels (as wages were to be paid in food grains). While generating employment, durable community assets were to be created which would strengthen the rural infrastructure and result in higher production and better living standard in rural areas. The idea was also to utilize thesurplus food grains for development of human resources and employment creation.

A total of 979.32 million mandays' employment was generated during the period from 1977—78 to 1979–80

(September). This scheme became very popular in the rural areas and came to be recognized as a major instrument of rural employment. A number of deficiencies were also noticed in the implementation of the Food for Work Programme including erratic disbursement of food grains as wages, delay in measurement ofearth work, non—durability of the assets created under the programme, inadequate technical supervision of works and the lack of proper supervision which led to dilution of technical requirement of the projects.

The FWP was restructured and renamed as National Rural Employment Programme (NREP) in October, 1980 as a culmination of previous experiences in this field. The programme became part of the VI Five Year Plan from April, 1981 andwas implemented as a Centrally—sponsored scheme on a 50:50 sharing basis between the Centre and States with the three—fold objectives of generation of additional gainful employment, creation of durable comunity assets and raising of the nutritional standards of the rural poor. The programme envisaged an outlay of Rs. 1,620 crore including the States' matching share during the VI Plan period to generate additonal employment opportunities to the extent of 300 to 400 million mandays per year, simultaneously creating durable community assets.

During the VI Plan, the total expenditure on implementation of NREP was Rs. 1,873 crore as against the outlay of Rs. 1,620 crore including the States'share. The target of employment generation as envisaged under the Plan was also achieved. The total employment generation during the period was 1,775.18 million mandays. The midterm appraisal of the VI Plan, however, pointed out that the hard core of rural poverty pertaining to employment opportunities particularly for the landless during the lean agriculture periods, (when work in agriculture is scarce) had to be tackled in a much more direct and special manner. It was, therefore, though that at least one member from each landless household should be provided employment up to 100 days in a year. With this end in view, the Rural Landless Employment Guarantee Programme (RLEGP) was launched in August, 1983, as a fully funded programme by the Central government and was implemented in additon to the National Rural Employment Programme covering the entire country.

During the VII Plan, an expenditure of Rs. 7,809.93 crore was made and 3,496.30 million mandays' employment was generated under NREP and RLEGP. While these two programmes have been able to exceed the financial and physical targets, it has not been possible to provide 100 days of employment to at least one member of each landless household in a year as envisaged under RLEGP.